Building Pedagogical Curb Cuts: Incorporating Disability in the University Classroom and Curriculum

Contents

Acknowledgements   vii
Chancellor's Preface   ix
Editors' Introduction   xi

I. Incorporating Disability in the Curriculum

Mainstreaming Disability: A Case in Bioethics   3
Anita Ho
Language Barriers and Barriers to Language: Disability   11
in the Foreign Language Classroom
Elizabeth Hamilton and Tammy Berberi
Including Women with Disabilities in Women and   21
Disability Studies
Maria Barile
Seeing Double   33
Ann Millett
Cinematically Challenged: Using Film in Class   43
Mia Feldbaum and Zach Rossetti
"Krazy Kripples": Using *South Park* to Talk   67
about Disability
Julia White
Teaching for Social Change   77
Kathy Kniepmann

II. Designing Instruction for Everyone

Nothing Special: Becoming a Good Teacher for All   89
Zach Rossetti and Christy Ashby

Tools for Universal Instruction   101
   Thomas Argondizza
"Lame Idea": Disabling Language in the Classroom   107
   Liat Ben-Moshe
Learning from Each Other: Syracuse University   117
and the OnCampus Program
   Cheryl G. Najarian and Michele Paetow

III. Students with Disabilities in the Classroom

Being an Ally   131
   Katrina Arndt and Pat English-Sand
Adapting and "Passing": My Experiences as a   139
Graduate Student with Multiple Invisible Disabilities
   Elizabeth Sierra-Zarella
"We're not Stupid": My College Years   147
as a Mentally Challenged Student
   Anthony J. Nocella, II
Crucial Communication Triangle: Students with   157
Disabilities, Faculty and Disability Support Services
   Sara Pace
Signs of Inclusion: Using Sign Language Interpreters   165
in the Classroom
   Jeremy L. Brunson
Legal Requirements for Students with Disabilities   177
and Universities
   Crystal Doody and Julie Morse

Resource Guide   185
   Liat Ben-Moshe

Contributors   201

Acknowledgements

The editors would like to thank all those who labored and assisted in the creation of the book.

First, we would like to acknowledge the tremendous efforts made by members of the Beyond Compliance Coordinating Committee, BCCC, in advocating for a learning environment that values human differences, a vision that is at the forefront of this book.

We express our sincere gratitude to Stacey Lane Tice of the Graduate School for her vision, her support and for her continuing work to improve graduate education.

Thanks are also due to Dr. John Mercer, Dean of the Graduate School, for his strong support of this pedagogical effort and his recognition of the importance of disability pedagogy.

We would also like to share our appreciation for the people on campus that regularly engage in conversation about this topic and the helpful advice they have given us. Our advisory board: Christy Ashby, Doug Biklen, Bob Bogdan, Beth Ferri, Nisha Gupta, Arlene Kanter, Maho Kasahara, Keonhee Kim, Zach Rossetti, Steve Simon, Horace Smith, Steve Taylor and Stacey Lane Tice.

Special thanks goes to Chancellor Nancy Cantor and Associate Chancellor Jo Thomas for their thoughtful preface and expressed commitment to promote diversity on our campus.

The Center on Human Policy at Syracuse University provided crucial support in the development of this book and its resource guide. In particular, we would like to thank Hank Pinkowski for creating the overall layout of the book. Additionally, we acknowledge the effort of our copy editor, Lori Foster, who read through multiple drafts of these works.

Finally we would like to give appreciation to all the wonderful authors who contributed to this book: Ann Millett, Elizabeth Hamilton, Tammy Berberi, Maria Barile, Kathy Kniepmann, Julia White, Zach Rossetti, Anita Ho, Christy Ashby, Thomas Argondizza, Cheryl G. Najarian, Michele Paetow, Katrina Arndt, Pat English-Sand, Elizabeth Sierra-Zarella, Anthony J. Nocella, II, Sara Pace, Jeremy L. Brunson, Crystal Doody and Julie Morse.

Without these efforts, this book would have never come to light. For all of us, it was truly a labor of love.

Liat Ben-Moshe, Rebecca C. Cory, Mia Feldbaum, and Ken Sagendorf

Building Pedagogical Curb Cuts: Incorporating Disability in the University Classroom and Curriculum

A preface by Nancy Cantor, Chancellor and President of Syracuse University

Older readers may remember the advent of curb cuts, created for pedestrians with wheelchairs, walkers, crutches or canes and so useful that you wondered why no one thought of them before. Younger readers could be excused for thinking they were intended for the strollers, bicycles, wheelbarrows, skateboards, roller blades, grocery carts, luggage carriers and lawnmowers that use them every day.

Building Pedagogical Curb Cuts challenges us to alter the fixed concrete sidewalks of our lives and practices, arguing persuasively that there are imaginative ways to include disability in our classrooms and in our lives, to the benefit of all.

Without minimizing the experiences of people with disabilities, it is also important to recognize that disability is fundamentally about difference, not impairment, inability or inadequacy.

We all use curb cuts. Disability, as the authors of this insightful book observe, is both fluid and contextual. One person may be blind at birth, another in old age. One might be disabled by genetics, another by a ski accident. Some disabilities are visable while others are hidden. The experience might last days, weeks or a lifetime.

The authors in this important and useful volume challenge us to move beyond restrictive, traditional methods of teaching, as well as exclusionary theoretical perspectives. They challenge us to create environments where the perspectives of all are taken into account, and they suggest many, many possibilities.

This collaboration is the work of the Beyond Compliance Coordinating Committee and the Future Professoriate Program of the Graduate School of Syracuse University. As an institution, Syracuse welcomes students with disabilities, recognizing that they bring with them a wealth of experiences, good and bad, that enrich our campus community and, as this book shows, give us many opportunities to innovate and improve higher education for everyone.

Editors' Introduction

Liat Ben-Moshe, Rebecca C. Cory, Mia Feldbaum and Ken Sagendorf

In her August 1, 2004 letter to the community, the new chancellor of Syracuse University, Dr. Nancy Cantor, asked, "Across disciplines, constituencies, and roles, how can we engage thoughtfully to make a difference? ... Who defines *the problem* ... and how do we talk to each other and listen respectfully?" In this book, we attempt to address these questions with regard to disability. What is disability? Who defines it? What does this mean for us here on a university campus or in our classrooms? Does it mean different things for students than for teachers? Finally, what can we do as individuals to create an environment where the perspectives of all are taken into account?

In trying to answer the chancellor's questions, we must first examine the meaning of the term "disability." Disability is often seen as a static category with clear boundaries between the disabled and the nondisabled. Upon closer examination, however, the fluidity of the label "disability" is evident. For example, consider people with age-related hearing loss who identify as nondisabled in relation to those have less hearing loss, but who identify with the Deaf community. Where is the line between them? What about someone who tests poorly in math, but is brilliant in art? Would that person count as disabled? Studies of individual cases reveal that disability is contextual.

To further complicate the definition, there is significant variation within the group that is identified as disabled. For instance, people with vision impairments and people with psychiatric labels fall into the same category, yet what do they have in common? Although contested in its meaning and value, the category "disabled" does legitimately exist. It is based on a commonality of experience, a shared history of oppression, and the identification as disabled by self or others. Similarities of experience and advocacy have created the disability rights movement, a movement based on full participation and autonomy for people labeled with disabilities. Scholarship and theory around disability developed from this movement. Activist and author James Charleton said, "having a disability is *essentially* neither a good thing nor a bad thing. It just is." (p. 167). Nonetheless there are multiple ways of understanding disability. This book seeks to examine the fluidity of the category of disability in the instructional setting.

This book is the result of a collaborative and interdisciplinary effort to examine how the university can better include the perspectives of scholars and students who have disabilities in the classroom. Through the combined efforts of the Beyond Compliance Coordinating Committee (BCCC) and the Graduate School, both of Syracuse University. BCCC is an advocacy organization of students working to create and support a positive climate for disability that values individual difference in all university settings. In the fall of 2003, the BCCC approached the Graduate School to present its vision and mission, and to gain support. The Future Professoriate Program (FPP) of the Graduate School took on the project of producing this book as part of its efforts and invited the editors of this book to participate in coordinating this effort. The FPP prepares graduate students for the full range of responsibilities they might assume as employees in higher education. The authors of this book come from a variety of disciplines and have engaged in disability scholarship, activism or accommodation in their classes.

The book is organized into three sections followed by a resource guide. Each of the articles discusses a different aspect of bringing the disability perspective and/or students with disabilities into the classroom. Anita Ho begins the section **Incorporating**

Disability into the Curriculum with, "Mainstreaming Disability: A Case in Bioethics." She encourages instructors to avoid marginalizing disability or using it as an "add on" to reading materials. She demonstrates her claim by using examples from bioethics courses. Elizabeth Hamilton and Tammy Berberi examine how disability is, or is not, taught as part of the foreign language curriculum in "Language Barriers and Barriers to Language: Disability in the Foreign Language Classroom." In her article, "Including Women with Disabilities in Women Studies," Maria Barile examines some of the benefits and problems of the intersection of disability studies and women studies. Ann Millett's "Seeing Double," examines ways of teaching about artistic representations of different bodies.

It is common to use popular culture to explore academic concepts. In "Cinematically Challenged: Using Film in Class," Mia Feldbaum and Zach Rossetti explore some of the most common tropes of film representations of disability and provide a film directory to help integrate disability into the classroom. Julia White, in her article, "'Krazy Kripples': Using *South Park* to Talk About Disability," deconstructs an episode of the popular adult cartoon television program, and models how cultural products such as television shows can be used to teach disability theory. In "Teaching for Social Change," Kathy Kniepmann uses media representations of disability to teach students about social participation and human dignity.

In **Designing Instruction for Everyone**, the authors discuss their experiences with teaching diverse groups of learners and demonstrate how advanced planning can create an accessible and challenging learning environment for all. In "Nothing Special: Becoming a Good Teacher for All," Zach Rossetti and Christy Ashby discuss how they create classrooms that are accessible to their students. Similarly, in "Tools for Universal Instruction," Thomas Argondizza outlines the principles of Universal Design that are the foundation for an accessible curriculum. Liat Ben-Moshe, in "Lame Idea: Disabling Language in the Classroom," examines how we, as instructors, should be mindful of our language since the terminology we use may perpetuate abelist stereotypes. This section concludes with "Learning from Each Other: Syracuse University and the OnCampus Program" by Cheryl G. Najarian and Michele Paetow. They discuss the experiences of two teachers who participated in the On Campus program at Syracuse University; a program that supports students labeled with cognitive disabilities in their experiences at the university.

In the section **Students with Disabilities in the Classroom**, the book explores the classroom experience from the perspective of students with disabilities. Each of these articles narrates a personal experience of a student or group of students in the classroom. In "Being an Ally," Katrina Arndt and Pat English-Sand discuss how they, as instructors and non-disabled students, have worked to ally themselves with the disability rights movement and support their peers who have disabilities. "Adapting and 'Passing': My Experiences as a Graduate Student with Multiple Invisible Disabilities" by Elizabeth Sierra-Zarella and "We're not Stupid: My College Years as a Mentally Challenged Student" by Anthony Nocella, II, chronicle two specific students' experiences in higher education. In "Crucial Communication Triangle: Students With Disabilities, Faculty, and Disability Support Services" by Sara Pace and in "Signs of Inclusion: Using Sign Language Interpreters in the Classroom" by Jeremy L. Brunson, the authors discuss aspects of collaboration among faculty, students and auxiliary service providers. Crystal Doody and Julie Morse's "Legal Requirements for Students with Disabilities and Universities" makes sense of the requirements for classroom accessibility and inclusion from an American legal standpoint. The book concludes with a resource guide to help readers find further resources for making classrooms inclusive and integrating the disability perspective into curricula.

This book is by no means a complete account of all pedagogical issues pertaining to disability. It cannot, and does not cover all disciplines, all disabilities or all topics; however, we feel that the information presented in this volume can be applied to most disciplines and all disabilities. We see this volume as a starting point. We invite you to engage with the content and ideas, to ask questions and to challenge yourselves and your colleagues to look at your curricula through the perspectives and ideas presented here.

References

Charlton, J.I. (1998). *Nothing About Us Without Us: Disability Oppression and Empowerment*. Berkeley: University of California Press.

I.
Incorporating Disability in the Curriculum

Mainstreaming Disability: A Case in Bioethics

Anita Ho

A student in my biomedical ethics class once asked why I required a textbook plus a reading packet. As she said, it would have been cheaper to simply buy one textbook. I told her that I had hoped to use only one textbook, but that unfortunately I was unable to find one that truly incorporates diverse perspectives, especially the disability perspective. My student's question gave me an opportunity to talk with the class about why certain perspectives are often left out of the academic and social/political debates. Some students confessed that they had not even noticed any gaps in the debates, even though, when asked, they acknowledged that disability perspectives were almost never brought up. Others suggested that certain perspectives were left out because they affect very few people in the society. One student, for example, suggested that race and disability issues are mostly of interest only to those who are of such minority status.

These responses are significant, especially since many of these students plan to pursue health-related careers that might involve working with people with disabilities. Disabled people and their families might have to rely on these students to advise them in decisions that affect the quality of their lives. In biomedical ethics, it is obvious that the disability perspective is an essential part of all aspects of the curriculum. However, it should not stop there. I challenge that a disability perspective should be incorporated into all classes in all disciplines, and not simply treated as a topic that is separate from other issues.

At our college, biomedical ethics is required or recommended for various health-related majors. Many of these students have worked with, or at least are being trained to work with, people with disabilities. However, the majority of them have no or little prior exposure to various disability perspectives. While these students, in general, believe in promoting social justice, many of them continue to hold stereotypical attitudes towards (people with) disabilities and hierarchical assumptions that come with various professional roles. These students presume an understanding of who does or does not have a disability, and believe that their role is to "help" the "vulnerable" people with disabilities. Even though many of these students have never engaged in serious discussions regarding disability with people who live with various circumstances, they have preconceptions about the meaning of having a disability, the quality of life of people with disabilities, and/or the respective abilities of people with different types and levels of characteristics.

It is not surprising that students continue to hold stereotypes and mistaken or biased views of (people with) disabilities. After all, the current curriculum has done little to dispel the stigma. In fact, it may be part of the problem. As previously mentioned, the "regular" curriculum and textbooks still neglect or marginalize the disability perspective. Recent attempts to promote diversity have resulted in more discussions of gender and racial issues, but the disability perspective remains neglected. Even bioethics textbooks rarely address disability issues. In those seldom cases where textbooks mention disability, they continue to employ a medical model of disability that characterizes disability as a defect that is inherent in the person with an impairment. These discussions rarely address social and political problems that "disable" many people. Rather, they focus on disability as a physical/mental inferiority that ought to be corrected by medical procedures. It is, therefore, not surprising that students in the mainstream curriculum continue to hold various stereotypes of (people with) disabilities.

Some have proposed closing the curriculum gap by adding "disability studies" or a disability component to various academic programs, but is this the answer? Certainly, if we think that disability is an area that is as important as, say, physiology, it seems desirable to expose students to various disability perspectives. In recent years, some larger universities have started offering majors or minors in disability studies. Some of them also offer disability studies courses as electives for students in various disciplines. However, because of limited resources and enrollment, many small, or even mid-size colleges and universities, do not have departments or even courses in disability studies. Even when such courses are available, not all students can take advantage of the opportunities. Many programs (for example, health-care professional programs) have strict schedules and little flexibility to add any other courses to their curricula.

Moreover, having separate courses on disability may continue to give mixed signals to students regarding the social and political meanings of disability. Separate courses may reinforce the message that disability is a "fringe" matter that is separate from our everyday experience and political reality. Gender studies, racial/ethnic studies, queer studies and disability studies are all important programs that have made significant contributions to equality in our society. However, many students assume that these subjects are "special studies" that are only of interest to those who fit certain profiles. Just as many assume that only "extreme feminists" enroll in women's studies, or that only people of color would want to take racial/ethnic studies, a majority of students still seem to think that disability studies is a field of narrow focus that is relevant only to students with disabilities or to others who wish to pursue careers in disability-related fields.

Given these concerns, I contend that a better alternative for introducing all students to diverse perspectives is to incorporate disability perspectives in "regular" classes. Incorporation of disability perspectives provides an opportunity for students who are unable or unwilling to take disability studies courses to learn about diverse perspectives. It provides students a venue to critically examine how various issues have important social and political implications on people with diverse characteristics. Moreover, disability becomes not just a topic, or an "alternative study." Rather, it becomes a part of our everyday existence that is relevant to all of us, whether we are in the health-care setting, a business environment or in any other field. We are all born with different characteristics and encounter various circumstances (e.g., injuries, sickness, old age), but our economic and social contexts continue to favor only select forms of existence. It is vital for students to understand, critically examine and challenge such structures in the main curriculum.

In promoting diverse perspectives, we also need to pay attention to *how* we incorporate disability issues. It is not enough that instructors include materials about disabilities. As previously mentioned, some textbooks do discuss disability issues, but they do so from an able-bodied bias, which can perpetuate various stereotypes regarding disability. An inclusive course must balance various perspectives and incorporate the voices of people with disabilities. Students need to critically examine how and why the existing structure may affect individuals of various characteristics and experiences differently.

Some may worry that incorporation of disability issues will distract students from the most important topics. Some instructors have told me that, just as it is often impossible to add an extra course to the curriculum, they have no time for a disability topic in their already-full schedules. I challenge the uncritical assumption that the current able-bodied curriculum is best, such that any change would compromise the quality of the learning. Some instructors mistakenly assume that incorporation of disability issues means that we must *replace* the mainstream topics with disability topics. However, as previously mentioned, disability is not an additional "topic" that is separate from other issues. It is not enough to spend a week "tackling" disability issues. Rather, disability perspectives are an important part of most topics. Many issues have important implications for people with and without disabilities. The strategy is not to replace "traditional topics" with "disability topics." Instead, the strategy is to examine or incorporate the disability perspective in these "traditional" topics.

Let us take biomedical ethics as an example. For most undergraduate courses and textbooks in this area, main topics include resource allocation, reproductive rights, research ethics, euthanasia and genetics. The problem in these courses is not that we leave out disability as one of the "topics." Rather, the problem is that, while resource allocation, genetics, and so on, affect everyone, discussions and case studies address only the social and political implications these issues may have on people without disabilities. The perspectives and experiences of people with disabilities are often neglected. When disability issues are raised, they are often addressed from able-bodied and biased perspectives. For example, when presenting issues of reproduction, euthanasia and genetics, many bioethicists focus only on autonomy while making assumptions of inferior lives for those who live with disabilities. Authors on these topics often hail various medical technologies as liberating remedies that promise better lives or an end to sufferings. They take ideas of reproductive freedom and well-being, which are often based on able-bodied stereotypes, for granted.

In the reading packet that my student wished she did not have to purchase, I included articles and discussions from the disability perspectives that help to challenge the ways we understand various concepts. While we still discussed "traditional" topics, we paid special attention to how these topics are often framed in the mainstream debate, including decisions about which voices are heard and marginalized respectively. For example, in our discussion of genetic testing, we examined how debates of autonomy and quality of life are often tied to the medical view of disability that neglects the oppressive nature of the social structure. These debates usually ignore various social and political implications that prenatal genetic diagnosis and selective abortion might have on people with disabilities. Our readings from various disability perspectives helped us to challenge the way we thought about parenting, "harm" to future generations and quality of life.

We easily incorporated the disability perspective into our discussion of euthanasia. When I took a poll at the beginning of the class, every student indicated that Dr. Kevorkian, who was convicted of second-degree murder for giving a lethal injection to a terminally ill man, did nothing morally wrong. As a philosopher who was used to discussing diverse perspectives, I was stunned by the absolute agreement among the students. When questioned, many students explained that sometimes one's quality of life could be so bad that death was preferable. Some cited examples from the hospitals or nursing homes where they worked with patients who were permanently paralyzed, terminally ill and/or in constant severe pain. I asked these students whether *they* thought these patients' lives were not worth living. Some of them nodded; others indicated that they simply would not want to live in such a state. They initially held the view that there could be objective and/or "medical" ways to determine one's quality of life, and were relieved that most of the articles in our textbook presented similar views. Most students initially had difficulty accepting the possibility that life with disabilities can still be fulfilling, or that social attitudes and availability of resources may be more relevant to the quality of life than "medical" conditions.

However, after reading articles from the disability perspectives and discussing various actual cases related to euthanasia and disability (Larry McAfee, Elizabeth Bouvia, Tracy Latimar, etc.), some students began to acknowledge that the ways they considered futility, ethics of euthanasia, withdrawal of treatment and resource allocations were affected by their able-bodied assumptions about well-being. They started to recognize how the social structure continues to unfairly favor certain forms of existence over others. One student, who thought one of her patients would be better off dead than alive in her current state, told me after class that she was embarrassed about her ignorance. She was worried that her negative attitude might have affected the way that her patient thought about her life.

It is unfortunate that I have not been able to find a textbook that truly embraces diverse perspectives. It appears that I will once again be using an additional reading packet for my next biomedical ethics class. After all, we cannot have a full understanding of various ethical implications of genetics and euthanasia without the disability perspective. Hopefully, one day all "mainstream" editors will realize the importance of diverse perspectives and will eliminate the need for an "extra" reading packet. As I said, disability is not an "additional" topic, but an important part of our everyday existence.

Anita Ho teaches at the College of St. Catherine in St. Paul, Minnesota.

Language Barriers and Barriers to Language: Disability in the Foreign Language Classroom

Elizabeth Hamilton
Tammy Berberi

The motivation for this article is the shared conviction that we as teachers have an ethical responsibility toward students with disabilities that surpasses the minimum legal requirement of reasonable accommodation. In foreign languages, minimal compliance has most often resulted in the exclusion of students with disabilities who are granted course waivers or substitution courses (in English) for beginning required foreign language sequences. At the other end of the curriculum, advanced students with disabilities who wish to pursue study abroad report that they are actively discouraged from doing so by study abroad offices and campus disability advocates alike; at best, substitute, on-campus experiences are offered.

Yet, when we as foreign language teachers are called to defend our vocation against threats of budget and program cuts, we argue quite convincingly that foreign language study is "fundamental" to the success of students, an "essential component" of a solid humanistic education. We champion foreign language study precisely because we know its classroom to be the ideal forum for fostering and practicing the thoughtful consideration of differences between people and cultures, within our own culture and within ourselves.

Disability is absent from our cours   aterials and

curricula. It is absent even though the experience of the body, like that of language, is universal—as much a part of each day as any activity we rehearse in our classrooms—and culturally specific, shaped by a multitude of factors ranging from family structure to the structure and priorities of local and national governments and from to local topography and infrastructure to religious and secular beliefs. Disability belongs in our foreign language classrooms because it exists everywhere, and because we still have a lot to teach each other about it, at home and abroad.

Advocacy in the classroom

As foreign language teachers, we can work individually and in concert to redress this double standard. We can start in our classrooms by recognizing first, that the full participation of students with disabilities does not necessarily entail extra work and second, that intrinsically normative teaching methods may give rise to exceptional needs in classrooms. We can develop and practice approaches to teaching that are based upon the principles of Universal Design in Instruction, draw upon a variety senses, and rely upon well-calibrated sequencing, frequent repetition, and a cyclical return to key concepts within a lesson. Universal Design—the concept of designing classrooms and curricula in such a way that they accommodate all learning styles, abilities and disabilities without the need for adaptation or special equipment— enables the fullest possible participation of all students (see **Model Lesson** that follows).

Following are some suggestions for achieving such a balance in classrooms:

- Develop a learning styles survey to encourage all students to reflect upon their learning strengths and weaknesses. (Beginners will be better prepared to assess after a few weeks of foreign language at a college pace.) Based on the information gathered in the surveys, create groups of students with complementary learning strengths so as not to alienate any one group of students from a particular activity: students will be better equipped to enable each other's success.

- To further acknowledge various learning styles, consider creating a variety of syllabi options and allowing students to choose which they prefer at the beginning of the semester. For example, option 1 might weigh all skills equally in calculating the grade. Option 2 might privilege reading and writing skills. Option 3 might privilege speaking activities and oral exams. This does not necessarily require extra tailoring to each student; all students complete all activities. Teachers simply keep records of the options students choose and calculate grades according to those choices. A set of options such as this might meet the needs of students who are dyslexic or dysgraphic, as well as those of students with hearing impairments who may not be able to participate fully in the interactive aspects of courses.

- Consider the adjustments to assessment tools. Can tests be administered orally, or can students complete written exams using voicing software such as Dragonspeak? Can one modality, such as speech, be substituted for another modality, such as writing? Perhaps listening can substitute for reading.

- Incorporate a variety of presentation modes for regular vocabulary and grammar lessons. Have students acquire and review new structures in reading, writing and speech. One day's vocabulary might be presented first through pictures, and then repeated by reading from the textbook. Next, students could review the words by writing them on the blackboard, incorporating them into a role play or choral reading, and summarizing them again in writing for homework. Engaging multiple modalities allows for fuller language acquisition in all students. Students with sensory or learning disabilities especially benefit from the variety of opportunities to participate and from the recursive review of material.

- Consider in advance of lessons what, if any, adaptive materials are necessary. Many types of information that teachers produce for printed handouts or write on the board can be made tactile for the blind student's repeated reference. Examples include definite and indefinite article charts; adjective endings; word order; conjugation rubrics; and graphs and data.

- Whenever possible, involve the entire class in creating adapted materials. If a student needs, for example, audio versions of material that is presented visually to other students, enlist students in the course to produce these audio files. The students will get practice reading aloud in the target language and be motivated to do well for their peer. The listener will have several versions recorded with different voices and intonations and at different speeds. Repetition will enable the student to anticipate vocabulary and practice pronunciation, phrasing and inflection.

Model Lesson: A German Class

Target
Third- or fourth-semester students, but may be adjusted for beginning-level students.

Goals
1. Practice the simple past tense.
2. Generate vocabulary.
3. Practice formulating questions.

4. Introduce Gebrauchslyrik or "everyday poetry," part of a German literary and artistic movement of the 1920s known as New Objectivity.

Materials
1. Copy of Richard Gessner's painting "Paris bei Nacht" (1927) or another picture of a distant couple in a café.
2. Copies of Erich Kästner's poem, "Sachliche Romanze."
3. A bag containing objects named in the poem, and other objects that one might associate with love or romance.

Technology
A Brailled copy of Erich Kästner's poem, "Sachliche Romanze."

Part I
     Distribute a copy of a café scene to half the students in the course, telling the others only that the scene takes place in a café. Students who do not have the picture formulate questions to find out what else the painting conveys. Their questions will naturally range from which objects and figures are portrayed, to the atmosphere and mood of the painting. Students with the picture will be compelled to focus their attention on the painting and begin to analyze it. They will likely become aware of far more details this way than they would if they were simply asked to describe the painting. Allow as much time as necessary for the questioners to form a mental picture.

Part II
     The other half of the class draws objects from the bag, without revealing them to their classmates. The students holding the selected objects must give clues to their identities, referring to tactile qualities, size, smell, or taste with examples of when or how they might use the items. This allows the class to reuse vocabulary generated from the first activity, and guides the discussion toward the present day.

Part III

Distribute copies of Kästner's poem and ask several students to read it aloud. Students evaluate the quality of the relationship portrayed in the poem and examine the language through which that relationship is illustrated. Students can continue to develop their abilities to formulate questions by assuming roles of figures in the poem or painting. What questions would one figure ask of the other? Next, ask students to step back out of character and follow up as a group in any number of ways or allow them to choose individually from a range of options. They can create questions to analyze the mood or style of either artwork or the relationship portrayed in it, and then record their analytical questions on paper, present them as a dialogue or role play, contribute to a whole class discussion or write an essay. These sequenced activities provide avenues for further development. The teacher's role is to help students select the avenues that best enable their growth.

This model lesson demonstrates Universal Design in Instruction in its seamless inclusion of students with low vision. All three segments de-emphasize the visual, first, by depriving half the class of the visual cue and, second, by pulling objects from a bag and encouraging description of a full range of attributes. Finally, the activity provides meaningful cultural content and a real context for information exchange and discussion.

Disability in course materials

As teachers, we must acknowledge the paucity of materials conveying positive personal experiences with disability, and introduce disability-related materials as much as possible. When we integrate images, vocabulary, texts, songs and films that represent disability, we do not simply appeal to a special population within our classes, but we convey valuable cultural information to all students. Like any other cross-cultural or linguistic concept, the complexity of disability is easily reduced to its component parts: visual aids and regalia. We should collect these as we come across them. Establish realistic contexts in which students can use new skills.

We should examine textbooks to determine where disability perspectives would be useful. In the introduction to *No Pity: People with Disabilities Forge a New Civil Rights Movement* (1993), National Public Radio journalist Joseph P. Shapiro claims there is a disability angle to every story he develops. The same may be said of every lesson. These supplements need not be complete, distinct lessons. Rather, they can be added where they seem thematically or grammatically useful. For example, a French teacher might logically teach the adjectives "deaf," "hearing impaired," "blind" and "visually impaired" along with other variable and invariable adjectives, and the word "wheelchair" along with the word "armchair" since a wheelchair is a "rolling armchair" (*un fauteuil roulant*) in French. A teacher could expand a textbook chapter devoted to the body, but limited to run-of-the-mill occasional ailments, by acknowledging physical, sensory, mental, and emotional varieties of illness, and by teaching such words as "crutches," "cane," "dyslexia" and, indeed, "disability." The Internet is useful for finding authentic texts in the target language devoted to disability and the relevant themes. For example,a text on adaptive sports might complement a lesson on sports and leisure activities. A lesson on historical monuments and buildings would be enriched with pictures of retrofitted accessibility, or the absence thereof, and a subsequent discussion of how accessible our classrooms, campuses and communities are (or are not).

This accessibility angle can be included in studies of society or geography in the target country. Students can examine accessibility abroad as a discrete topic or in preparation for study abroad. Teachers can share pictures and experiences of students who have studied abroad in the past, and use these resources to make dis-abled students aware of some of the obstacles they might need to negotiate.[1] As an exercise in letter writing or telephoning, students can contact (or prepare to contact) hotels, museums, or other travel destinations to inquire about accessibility and investigate alternative modes of transportation. Ann M. Moore's *The Insider's Guide to Study Abroad* (2000) and the Access Abroad site at the University of Minnesota are good places to start.[2] (http://www.umabroad.umn.edu/access)

Disability in the arts is another interesting topic for students to study in their target languages. Film, drama, fiction and memoir are all rich sources for learning about living with disabilities. Literary and artistic works teach us about human life and identity because they require us to interpret human appearance, speech and action.

Advocacy beyond the classroom

New faculty members may be tempted to postpone developing the tools of advocacy until they encounter disabled students in their classrooms, but expertise and commitment to pedagogy are essential components of the advocacy network that teachers and students develop together. There are several ways new teachers can be proactive in developing strong networks:

- Forge a collegial relationship with the instructional technologists on campus. Spend an afternoon getting hands-on experience using the resources available, both assistive and for language learning. Test voicing technologies and screen readers to determine whether these tools are functional in particular foreign languages. Find out whether a Brailler is available. Determine whether specific diacritical marks can be Brailled automatically,or whether additional adjustments must be

---

[1] We thank Elizabeth Emery, assistant professor of French at Montclair State University, for the fabulous idea of using pictures to convey a different environment, and for many other ideas she offers in her unpublished paper, "*Cédez le passage*: Traveling in France with a Disability."

[2] Forthcoming at the time of publication is Rick Steves and Ken Plattner's *Rick Steves' Accessible Europe 2004* (Avalon Travel Publishing), which the authors have not yet had occasion to review.

made. Ask whether satellite programming is subtitled or close captioned. Find out whether there is a wheelchair accessible computer station in the lab. If the textbook publisher does not provide an alternative format, find out what formats the instructional technology support department routinely provides.

- Forge an equally collegial relationship with the office that provides services to disabled students to become aware of the range of accommodations that are available to students, and the related policies and procedures. Find out which programs the office supports to foster advocacy campus-wide. Awareness of these issues better equipts teachers to guide students in forging support networks.

- Visit the office that handles study aboard programs to gauge the staff's willingness to support disabled students. determine whether disabled students have traveled abroad in the past. Find out whether the office offers advice or experience about planning accessible trips. Also ask whether funds are available for disabled student travelers, either to purchase equipment (like lightweight titanium wheelchairs) that would make travel feasible, or to subsidize extra costs associated with disabilities such as taxi rides or an American Sign Language interpreter.

There is much work left to do in exploring the intersection of disability and foreign languages, and all contributions to advocacy are worthwhile and essential to the success of students as well as the future of the field. In 2003, we authors created a listserv, DISFL@oberlin.edu, to facilitate collaboration and discussion. We encourage teachers to contact us to take part in this ongoing discussion to compare methods, practices and policies and to share strategies and resources.

Tammy Berberi teaches French at the University of Minnesota.

Elizabeth Hamilton teaches German at Oberlin College.

Including Women with Disabilities in Women & Disability Studies

Maria Barile

In defining feminist pedagogy, theorist Linda Brinskin (1990) suggests three basic premises: she states first that, "Feminist pedagogy starts from the acknowledgement of women's oppression and speaks to the gendered characters..." She then states, "...to develop a feminist pedagogy one must unravel the contradictions of women's experience (p. 1)." Lastly, she discusses power roles in student-teacher relationships.

I propose that these three premises are equally applicable to women studies with respect to the inclusion of issues concerning women with disabilities. The proposal for identifying exclusion and indexing inclusion can be equally applied to the emerging disability studies. Herein, I will suggest other ideas that need to be explored and built into feminist pedagogy to provide diversity and inclusion. The process that feminist pedagogy must adopt has to be inclusive of both theory (teaching and research) and of practices in which we engage in our daily lives.

Pedagogical Exclusion

There are four major influences on pedagogical exclusion: 1) non-flexible requirements set up by programs, 2) the restrictive traditional methods of teaching, 3) exclusionary theoretical perspectives and 4) exclusionary instructional materials.

Much like the disability movements and women's movements of the 1970s and 1980s, disability studies and women studies are most often lacking in scholarship that informs us of theoretical and practical realities of and about women with disabilities. Specifically, the curricula lacks knowledge constructed from various disabled women's positions. Such constructions must be subjective and varied since disablement (both body and social) is experienced differently by various groups. Areas of difference that breed imbalances in the construction of disablement, for example, include those between men and women (Morris, 1993); between those who become disabled at different stages of life; among those who have different political and philosophical positions; among those whose views or understandings of body politics differ; and between those who perceive their disabilities as illnesses or physical limitations, and those who hold more socially constructed /political understandings of their realities.

The few courses directly about women with disabilities, emerging primarily from women studies, provide only an overview of the complexity of disabled women's realities. Either the research and instructional material used is not always a direct product of the lives of women with disabilities, or these materials focus on a "uni-view"—an often accepted dominant view about disability within women studies. Feminist scholar Jenny Morris (1993) maintains that feminist research cannot add women with disabilities without proper analysis, just as women's issues could not simply be added as subject matter in male-dominated scholarship. Feminist scholarship that simply adds disabled women to its existing curriculum or to its research as another element of diversity without proper context is, in effect, furthering (unintentional as it may be) the notion that women with disabilities are only an afterthought. This results in the omission of specific issues that concern women with disabilities in areas such as reproductive rights and violence against women.

Identifying Core Contradictions

In the 1940s and 1950s, students in medicine and health-related fields were taught about women's issues as "medical issues (Ehreneich & English, 1979)." Similarly, the issues of "impaired bodies" have been taught for years in disciplines such as medicine, rehabilitation and medical ethics (Hahn, 1991, Amundson, 1992). Teaching exclusively about "impaired bodies" from rehabilitation and individualistic approaches is not what disability studies is about (Linton, p. 124). Linton points out that disability studies adds a critical dimension to "pre-existing thinking about issues in civic and pedagogical culture (p. 118)." A curriculum of disability studies would look at issues of disablement from social justice perspectives and encourage students to critique existing policies and practices and alternative scholarly perspectives and disciplines. In philosophy, for example, the historical significance given to "normal" vs. "diversity" of bodies and minds is at the core of the oppression of women with disabilities and non-disabled women (Sampson, 2003; Tremain, 2001; Silver, 1998). New scholarship in these areas can be the nexus in which women with disabilities and non-disabled women can find common ground.

Women studies scholarship informs us that the traditional style of teaching did not include, and often excluded, women's learning patterns. By leaving out the daily experiences of women as housewives, mothers, etc., pedagogy often excluded women as learners and teachers. For example, in restrictive academic environments requiring intensive study for specific examinations given on set dates with no regard for the circumstances in the lives of learners, women who were unable to study because they were caring for sick children at home were being penalised. This is equally true of students with disabilities who come into school systems that have no adaptation. Often these students are penalised for not keeping up with students who need no adaptations. In the language of the social model of disability, these situations are problems of the individualistic approach, in which the individual must adapt to a 'disabling environment' (Oliver, 1996).

Other factors that impede inclusion are courses in which the techniques are entirely directed from a male-constructed knowledge of the world, a construction in which women and women's contributions are rarely mentioned (Oakley, 1981; Vickers, 1982). Even within most women studies and disability studies programs, the previous example of the student/mother can easily become real for women with disabilities. The program is designed with a social construct of non-disabled women in mind, or from a disabled-male perspective; very little is presented to students about the lives of disabled women. For example, women studies and political science courses often make mention of women's suffrage in America, yet rarely include the fact that Helen Keller marched next to non-disabled women in many liberation marches (Herrmann, 1999). These factors can emerge only if gender analysis and teaching methods are implemented from alternative viewpoints. We must look at the locus of the problem from different perspectives, analyzing variables such as the lives of women as mothers, victims/survivors in a non-egalitarian society and the imbalance of power from a socio-political perspective (Malhotra, 2003; Tremain, 2001; Silver,1998; Barnes, 2002). The challenge for any instructor is to find facts that will both inform and intrigue students, so that they can further expand theoretical knowledge.

Issues of Power

A more contentious point explored by Briskin (1988) regarding women in women studies is the issue of power. Briskin cites bell hooks with regards to the relationships between students and teachers and issues of power:

> To have a revolutionary feminist pedagogy we must first focus on the teacher-student relationship and the issue of power. How do we as feminist teachers use power in a way

that is not coercive, dominating? Many women have difficulty asserting power in the feminist classroom for the fear that to do so would be to exercise domination. Yet we must acknowledge that our role as teacher is a position of power over others. We can use that power in ways that diminish or in ways that enrich and it is this choice that should distinguish feminist pedagogy from ways of teaching that reinforces domination. (p. 29)

Teachers with disabilities are, at this point in time, among the first generation; for them and their students, the challenge is to understand the disparity or "flip-side" of power. Disabled instructors may be, on the one hand, in a position of greater power within the classroom, and still perhaps in other areas of their lives be in positions of lesser "perceived power." Still, such individuals have both the challenge and the privilege of grounding a new generation.

In considering the flip-side of the power issue, teachers must acknowledge the historical positions assigned to disabled persons as 'inferior,' 'having lives not worthy of living' (Morris, 1991). These historical positions may influence how both students and faculty perceive the professor with a disability. There may also be differences worth considering between a newly hired professor with a disability and a professor who already has a teaching position and becomes disabled. What will be the interaction and expectation of the two different professors? Will her or his knowledge be recognised for its own merits?

The newly hired professors with disabilities have several challenges. First, like all academics, they must prove the ability to teach. Like in any other job, disabled individuals have the responsibility of acknowledging the usual discomfort that may be present both with colleagues and students. Women and members of visible minorities are somewhat more prevalent in the current generation of academia; therefore, both students and faculty are more comfortable with their presence. Due to this inclusion of women and visible minorities, the subject matter of courses they teach becomes practical and not just theoretical. The presence of professors with disabilities likewise enriches students' learning experiences.

Toward Pedagogy of Distinctive Feminist Standpoint on Disability

Feminist pedagogy can play an important role in the inclusion of disability epistemology. To do so, it must insert "theoretical curb-cuts" (elements of theory that identify and connect the social/political and personal ways in which lives of women with disabilities are similar and simultaneously different from each other and from those of non-disabled women) and physical and technological access (Barile & Michèle, 2000). At the planning stage of their courses, professors must incorporate methods and theories that are in-sync with feminist principles of equality, and must be inclusive of diverse styles of learning concerning that content. As Mary Mahowald (1998) puts it:

> A feminist standpoint imputes privileged status to non-dominant perspectives not because those perspectives are more valid or more accurate (although sometimes they are) than the dominant perspective but because nondominant perspectives are typically missing from the perspective that dominates society at large. (p. 210)

Women's life experiences differ depending on their positions within given social structures. In the case of women with disabilities, there is the experience of cumulative oppression constructed from two incongruent viewpoints. Subject matter for courses must include these social and practical ramifications of the reality of women with disabilities. For instance, it must address mothers with disability-specific issues that cannot be met by services as they are presently structured. An example of the benefits of such inclusion involves the study of economics and poverty among women. An economic analysis of poverty for women with disability not only implies lower income, but also brings to light several other issues. Elwan's (1999) report on poverty informs us that:

> Disability rates for women seem to be higher than those for men in developed countries, and lower in developing countries. Lower female rates may indicate that severe impairments may be male-dominated, and/or females with disabilities may be under-reported or may receive less care and die sooner. For the childbearing age groups, female rates tend to be slightly higher, possibly because of ill health resulting from too many pregnancies, inadequate health and medical care, and poor nutrition." (p.5)

Moreover, this report also links gender to poverty and health issues:

> In some communities, disabled girls receive less care and food, and have less access to health care and rehabilitation services and fewer education and employment opportunities. They also tend to have lower marriage prospects than disabled men, and can be at risk of being abused physically and mentally. (p.18)

Any economic analysis must factor in expenditures due to disabling social structures that require additional materials to fulfill basic needs such as adapted housing and technologies to adapt disabling workplaces (Barile, 2002). Elwan's report found that once the extra disability-related costs were factored in, "The proportion [of disabled people living under the poverty line] increased to almost a half (p. 23)." In researching or teaching about human reactions to any disabling situation and/or disabling environment, we must take gender into account as an individual variable that interacts and produces specific results. Human geography tells us that space can either free restrict individuals' movements. Some empirical questions may be: how does the inaccessible space hinder safety for women with disabilities? How does that affect choice for disabled women in various parts of the world? (Chouinard, 1997; Imrie, 1996).

Feminist pedagogy must include specific voices of women with disabilities in all bodies that determine curricula for women studies and disability studies, both in teaching and in conducting research. One of the objectives of disability studies/women studies should be to dispel the notion that disabled people/women are objects and that actions are performed upon them. In the case of education, we must stop using people with disabilities exclusively as passive objects for learning. Educators, disabled or not, must include the perspectives of women and/or men who live the reality of disability using a variety of modes in the curriculum, not just in the form of videos in which students and teachers speak in abstract terms. The participation of women with disabilities compels discussion in real terms; therefore, bringing in women with disabilities from various viewpoints on disabled living would be ideal. Bringing in non-disabled representatives is not the same as bringing in people with disabilities. These two distinctive standpoints—living with a disability and living/working with people with disabilities—produce two different perceptions of reality, each with merits of its own. It is necessary that questions of power between these two groups be addressed.

Like instructors in women studies, in black/African-American studies and in other studies involving oppressed groups, people with disabilities who choose to teach are driven by the search for epistemological, ontological journey of ideological discovery. Thus, their presence in departments needs to be encouraged whenever possible. Such outreach can extend beyond the classroom. Universities can advance scholarship of and about women with disabilities by conducting co-operative research that includes women with disabilities as primary researchers, collaborators and partners in studies about women's lives.

The academic world must struggle to promote diversity of view points when research and teaching is based on the dominant view of any given moment, or when research hypotheses and analyses are based on funding that promotes a dominant position. To do otherwise will not service the students or society.

Disability studies and women studies have both the obligation and privilege of learning from the lives and experience of women with disabilities, and of including them as educators. Their participation would assist students, disabled or not, in critically questioning conventional knowledge about elements that have historically promoted oppression of persons with disabilities including disabling environments and policies along with the roles of the impaired bodies and language.

Maria Barile is a disability activist and a co-founder of Dis-Abled Women's Network Canada and its local affiliate Action des femmes handicapées (Montréal).

References

Amundson, R. (1992). Disability handicap and the environment. *Journal of Social Philosophy*, 23 (1), 105.

Barile, M. (2002, November). Individual-systemic violence: Disabled women's standpoint. *Journal of International Women's Studies,* 4(1), 1.

Barile, M. (2003). Globalization and ICF eugenics: Historical coincidence or connection? The more things change the more they stay the same. *Disability Studies Quarterly,* 23(2), 223.

Barile, M., & Michèle, M. (2000). *Comment rendre le féminisme accessible a Montréal / How to render feminism accessible in Montreal.* Montreal: La Table de groupes des femmes de Montreal (TGFM).

Barnes, C. & Oliver M., Barton L. (2002). Disability the Academy and inclusive society. In Barnes, C., Oliver M.& Barton L. (Eds.), *Disability Studies Today*. Malden, MA.: Polity Press.

bell hooks (1988). Toward a revolutionary feminist pedagogy. *Talking Back*. Toronto: Between Lines, 52.

Brinskin, L. (1990). *Feminist Perspectives féministes. Feminist Pedagogy: Teaching and learning liberation*. Canadian Research Institute for the Advancement of Women: Institue Canadien sur des recherches sur les femmes Ottawa.

Chouinard. V. (1997). Making space for differences: Challenging ableist geographers. *Environment and Planning D: Society and Space*, 15, 379-390.

Ehreneich, B .& English, D.(1979). *For Her Own Good: 150 Years of the Expert Advise to Women*. Doubleday, New York: Anchor Press.

Elwan, A. (1999). *Poverty and disability a survey of the literature*. Retrieved from the World Wide Web: www.worldbank.org/HDNet/HDdocs.nsf/View+to+Link+WebPages/

Hartsock, N. (1998). *The Feminist Standpoint Revisited & Other Essays*. Boulder, Co.: Westview Press.

Hahn, H. (1991) Theories and Values: Ethics and Contrasting Perspectives on Disability. In Marinelli, P. & Dell Orto, R. (Eds.), *The Psychological & Social Impact of Disability*. New York: Springer Publishing.

Herrmann, D (1999). *Helen Keller: A Life*. Chicago: University of Chicago Press.

Imrie, R. (1996). *Disability and the City*. New York: St Martin Press.

Linton, S. (1998). *Claiming Disability: Knowledge and Identity*. New York: New York University Press.

Mahowald, M. (1998). A feminist standpoint. In Silver, A. & Wasserman Mahowald, M. (Eds.), *Disability, Difference, and Discrimination: Perspective on Justice in Bioethics and Public Policy.* New York: Rowman and Littlefield.

Malhotra, R. (2003, Spring). The duty to accommodate unionized workers with disabilities in Canada and the United States: A counter-hegemonic approach. *Journal of Law & Equality,* 2, (1), (92-155). Available on the World Wide Web: http://www.jle.ca/files/v2n1/TOC.pdf

McCalla V. (1982). Memories of ontological exile: The methodological rebellions of feminist research. In Fin G. & Miles, A. (Eds.), *Feminism in Canada from Pressure to Politics.* Montreal: Black Rose, 27.

Meekosha, H. (1998). Body battles: Bodies, gender and disability. In Tom Shakespeare (Ed.), *The Disability Reader.* New York: Cassell, 177.

Morris, J. (1993, spring). Feminism and disability. *Feminist Review,* 43.

Morris, J. (1991). *Pride Against Prejudice: A Personal Politics of Disability.* London: The Women's Press.

Morris, J. (1992). Personal is political: A feminist perspective on researching disability. *Disability and Society,* 7(2), 157.

Oliver, M. (1996). *Understanding Disability: From Theory to Practice,* Houndmills, Basingstoke Hampshire: Macmillan Press Ltd.

Oakley, A. (1981). *Subject Women.* Toronto: Random House of Canada Ltd.

Sampson, F. (2003, spring). Globalization and the inequality of women with disabilities. *Journal of Law & Equality*, 2(1), 92. Available on the World Wide Web at http://www.jle.ca/files/v2n1/TOC.pdf

Silvers, A. (1998). "Reprising Women's Disability: Feminist Identity Strategy and Disability Rights." *Berkeley Women's Law Journal"* 13: 81-116.

Tremain, S. (2001). On the government of disability. Social Theory and Practice. *Special Issue Embodied Values: Philosophy and Disabilities* Vol. 27(4).

Wendell, S. (1996). *The Rejected Body: Feminist Philosophical Reflections on Disability*. New York: Routledge.

Seeing Double

Ann Millett

A course in social theory and cultural diversity is a requirement for undergraduates at the University of North Carolina at Chapel Hill. The cultural studies program sponsors such 80-level courses in several departments, including communication studies, sociology, anthropology, and international studies. All are designed to introduce students to fundamental theories of gender, race, ethnicity, class and sexuality and each is tailored to the specific discipline. I teach such a course through the university's art department. However, my course, Art 80, is unique in that it was I teach a modern art history course (Art 80) at the University of North Carolina at Chapel Hill that fulfills a requirement for all undergraduates in social theory and cultural diversity. Our university program in cultural studies sponsors such 80-level courses in several departments – communication studies, sociology, anthropology, and international studies – all designed to introduce students to fundamental theories of gender, race, ethnicity, class, and sexuality and each tailored to the specific discipline. My course was the first of its kind to survey modern/contemporary social and identity theories through the lens of visual culture.

My goals in the course are to engage disability studies perspectives to interrogate discursive and visual representations of all kinds of bodies. I guide class discussion on readings and related images to suggest strategies for classroom visual analysis using the framework of disability studies. This semester, I am focusing on representation of the body as a theme to connect written and visual materials. The body and the figurative traditions of art serve as a useful sites for centering discussions of identity, self/other dynamics, dominant and resistant ideologies, and the politics of visual representation. Because of my research and pedagogical interests, as well as personal experiences as a disabled woman, disability studies factors greatly in course readings, examples, and discussions.

Disability studies focuses intensely on bodies and their roles in social dynamics and, importantly for this course, contradicts assumptions about what bodies mean and do. For example, the discipline shakes up the premises of "normal" and "abnormal" bodies, questioning conventional narrative and representation in ways that resonate with modern/contemporary social theories and artwork. The perspectives of disability studies perspectives investigate the role of body in identity and social formation, examine the numerous, and often conflicting, frameworks in which the body is represented in society, and interrogate cultural metaphors for the body. Disability studies engages diverse perspectives on how the body may be a site, target, and vehicle for ideology and power, providing rich grounds for course materials.

My goals in the course are to engage disability studies perspectives to interrogate discursive and visual representations of all kinds of bodies. This essay illustrates how I guide class discussion on readings and related images to suggest strategies for classroom visual analysis using disability studies frameworks.

One rich discussion generates from "The Quasimodo Complex: Deformity Reconsidered (1996)," a psychoanalytic account of facial disfigurement by from theologian and clinician Jonathan Sinclair Carey. The 's article(1996) "The Quasimodo Complex: Deformity Reconsidered", a psychoanalytic account of facial disfigurement that discusses discusses traditions in literature, art, and film that cast characters with facial "abnormalities" as evil and tragic and as metaphorical for social and psychic disorder. In my class, we look at trans-historical examples of portraiture and caricature in which distortions of the body and facial features in particular connote personality characteristics, most often dubious ones. This leads to consideration of how appearance matters in daily life and and the role of bodies in cultural metaphors versus everyday lived experiences.

We also consider how pervasive representation constructs social identities and instills social limitations on and discriminations against those with visible physical deviations from contextual standards for "normal." I ask students if the subject of Carey's article is "disabled." This allows students to confront their own definitions of disability, leading some to articulate that the subject may be disabled due to social construction as "abnormal" and due to oppression based on stereotypes surrounding his body, rather than impaired in a physiological sense of limitation. I might then A student than asked is whether obese people could be considered disabled, leading to a discussion of the label "disabled," to whom it applies to, and what it means.

Rosemarie Garland-Thomson's article "Seeing the Disabled: Visual Rhetorics of Disability in Popular Photography," (2001), included in the recent "canon" of disability studies, usefully ties together themes of social construction with visual mediation and representation, focusing on a variety of photographs of visibly disabled people.[1] In my class, I show examples of early clinical photography and twentieth century documentary, asking students to analyze how these photographs frame bodies in their formal techniques. We consider how they construct certain bodies as "abnormal" or physically deviant and diseased through photographic conventions. With images of amputation, again facial deformities, and poor immigrants,

---

[1] She discusses important assumptions of photography as "real" or displaying truth and evidence, which relates well to an excerpt I have students read from John Tagg's *Burden of Representation* (1988) (1988), in which Tagg performs a Foucaudultian analysis of early photography as an instrument for ideological exercises of power and surveillance, mainly over bodies.

for example, some students begin to question what makes them
often disturbing, whether the reactions are triggered by the bodies
themselvesy itself or the way how the photographs represent them.
Because photographs mediate the "real" and construct
representation through particular aesthetics and conventions,
Garland-Thomson maintains, photographs of disabled people not
only reflect, but also produce discourses and evaluations of
disability in society. [2]

Garland-Thomson's essay serves as a practical introduction
to how to analyzing ze photographs in general, as she walks the
reader through specific categories of the predominant discourses
on disability that she sees operating in the images: the wondrous,
the sentimental, the exotic, and the realistic. (p. 339) Particularly
significant for me, as I stress to students throughout the semester
that visual images are never clear-cut nor closed in meaning, is
that Garland-Thomson writes that her rhetorical
categories necessarily overlap in each image. Further, she offers
that each image may be viewed as both a "positive" (affirmative)
and "negative" (derogatory) representation of disability. This helps
explain suggests how the most provocative, memorable, and
widely circulated images in society are often the least
straightforward, although her analysis of specific examples, I feel,
leans towards criticism of them.

This may have to do with her specific thesis; the visual
examples presented, despite their diverse rhetoricss, socio-
historical contexts, and motivations, are all popular or commercial
representations of disabled people created by non-disabled
people;, and her agenda is to investigate terrogate how audiences,
mainly non-disabled audiences, read them. She poignantly
intersects the "gaze," —a significant subject of theoretical inquiry

[2] Her arguments and visual analyses connect with a variety of positions covered
in class about ideologies and aesthetics, including those of Karl Marx (1999)
(1999), Walter Benjamin (1999) (1999), and art historian Timothy J. Clark
(1992) (1992). In particular I ask students to consider Clark'ss' assertion that
ideology naturalizes visual representations (p. p. 43) in relationship to Garland-
Thomson's examples, and how representations might also, in turn, naturalize
ideology.

in visual cultural analyses, particularly for feminist and post-colonial agendas—, with the everyday notion of "the stare," which she names as particular to the experiences of visibly disabled people. She argues that the stare, sanctioned and exacerbated by the medium of photography, articulates distance and difference between disabled bodies on display and a non-disabled viewing public. This stare/gaze, according to Garland-Thomson, constructs disability as inferior and oppressed. I ask students if they agree. Could staring be a mode for productive interaction between disabled and non-disabled people, or could the act of viewing photography, or film and performance be such a mode? Does staring/gazing or /visually representing the other always make the subjects them "Other," in a display of dominance and exploitation?

Why and how does Garland-Thomson use her specific examples, and could her rhetorics extend to visual analysis of images of disability in "fine art" photography?[3] What discourses on disability, or physical "abnormality" operate in them and who has right to represent the "Other?"? How *should* they do so? Looking at specific images, such as Arbus's *Mexican Dwarf (a.k.a Cha Cha) in His Hotel Room* (1970), we consider how form, focus, composition, and iconography frame the dwarf in comparison with and divergence from conventional images of dwarfs in royal portraiture, freak shows, documentary photography, and popular culture.

If visual representation necessarily contains harmful cultural baggage, and if images are sometimes the predominant means for the non-disabled to experience disabled people, as Garland-Thomson points out, what are the arguments for and consequences of not representing or concealing representations? In Arbus's photograph, the dwarf boldly and ambiguously, indeed flirtatiously, stares back, leading to discussion of how the gaze/stare might be multi-directional and potentially instigate

---

[3] Such as the work of Lewis Hine, August Sander, Joel-Peter Witkin, and Diane Arbus.

optimistic social interactions and transgressions of spectator/spectacle distancing.

As the course progresses, I show my students many works by artists who make self-representational images— who put themselves on display—, such as the late artist Bob Flanagan, whose "sadomasochistic" performances and video installations address his experiences with the chronic and fatal disease cystic fibrosis, and Renée Cox, who photographs herself as a range of personas quoting pseudo-pornographic and popular images of black women. One image in particular, by Lyle Ashton-Harris in collaboration with Cox, features her posing as a postmodern Hottentot Venus, revisiting the history of Sarah Baartman, a woman from the Ivory Coast who was displayed as a medical specimen and sexualized freak show spectacle in late nineteenth-century England.

I also introduce Sander Gilman's "Black Bodies, White Bodies: Toward an Iconography of Female Sexuality in Late Nineteenth-century Art, Medicine, and Literature," (1986) in which he analyzes parallel constructions of the Hottentot Venus and the image of the nineteenth century prostitute (a repeated presence in modern painting, especially Edouard Manet's iconic Olympia, 1863, 1863)) as social deviants, specifically marked by physical (genital) disfigurement. Again Rreferencing Lorde, Tagg, Garland-Thomson, and Foucault, we may discuss science and art as ideological in their diagnosis and classification of "abnormality" based on physical deviation from standard conventions, as well as their implication in social discrimination against many groups. These specific instances become illustrations for the larger themes of disillusionment with scientific "progress" and universal truths that saturates modern social theory. Disability studies perspectives on the body synthesize fundamental modern/contemporary theories of identity and society with analysis of relevant visual images.

My pedagogical approach to visual analysis of body images is to push students toward "seeing double": taking notice of what is beyond the apparent or immediately assumed; reading against the grain, or, in opposition to the dominant narrative; perceiving both subjectivity and agency emerging from conventionally exploitative images, while at the same time interrogating those conventions, contexts, and receptions of images. I encourage students to trouble binary oppositions and recognize them as necessarily co-dependent, to interpret images as potentially botboth empowering and objectifying, affirmative and derogatory, and to see how all images convey mixed messages. I also work to create an environment where students feel free to express opinions and receive constructive criticism; however, yet because of the nature of the subjects, things inevitably get personal.

When students become animated about issues and relate personal experiences, particularly in identifications like Lorde's (outside of social categories), these are the richest moments. I also consider my own personal investment with the material, particularly as a disabled instructor engaging disability studies. As a scooter-user and visibly limb-impaired instructor, I balance my role as disabled person in a position of power with an attempt to avoid constructing myself as an "expert" on disabilities and other disabled or marginalized peoples. I try to be humble and open-minded to all perspectives and never present myself as an "expert," although I believe no instructor can, nor should, claim to be "objective." I have found myself challenged by issues that hit close to home, and I am sure at times I have become noticeably uncomfortable addressing personal matters in front of a group, especially one that takes notes and may reuse my thoughts in their papers.

I am, however, quite pleased I am pleased when students remark that disability studies is refreshingly new course material for them (although regretful that they haven't experienced it elsewhere) and that they find many of the perspectives engaging and liberating in their contentions with mainstream standards. The body does prove to be a provocative and multi-faceted, yet approachable theme for the course. Students hopefully learn to think critically, challenge popular beliefs, and ask good questions.

Further, they may even be impelled to question themselves and their conceptions of the roles of their own and others' bodies.

Ann Millett teaches at the University of North Carolina at Chapel Hill.

References

Benjamin, W.(1999). Art, war, and fascism. In Lemert, C. C. (Ed.), *Social Theory: The Multicultural and Classic Readings* (2nd ed.), p (pp. 255-257). Boulder, CO: Westview Press.

Carey, J.S. (1996). The Quasimodto complex: deformity reconsidered." In Donley, C.C. and Buckley, S. (Eds.), *The Tyranny of Normal: An Anthology*, (pp. 27-50). Kent, OH: Kent State University Press.

Clark, T.J. (1992). The painting of modern life. In F. Frascina & J. Harris (Eds.), *Art in Modern Culture: an Anthology of Critical Texts*, (pp. 40-50). New York: HarperCollins Publishers, Inc.

Lorde, A. (1984). The transformation of silence into language and action. In *Sister Outsider*, (pp. 40-44). Santa Cruz, CA: Crossing Press.

Garland-Thomson, R. (2001). Seeing the disabled: visual rhetorics of disability in popular photography. In P. K. Longmore & L. Umansky (Eds.), *The New Disability History: American Perspectives*, (pp. 335-222). New York: New York University Press.

Gilman, S. (1986). Black bodies, white bodies: toward an iconography of female sexuality in late nineteenth-century art, medicine, and literature. In J. Gates, Henry Louis (Ed.), *"Race," Writing, and Difference,* (pp. 223-261). Chicago: University of Chicago Press.

Marx, K. (1999). Camera obscura; Class struggle; and The fetishism of commodities. In Lemert, C. C. (Ed.), *Social Theory: The Multicultural and Classic Readings* (2nd ed.), (pp.36-40 and 59-60). Boulder, CO: Westview Press.

Tagg, J. (1988). *The Burden of Representation: Essays on Photographies and Histories*. Basingstoke, Hampshire: Macmillan Education.

Cinematically Challenged: Using Film in Class

Mia Feldbaum
Zach Rossetti

> *"The cultural representation of people with disabilities affects us all. In the broadest possible sense, it affects our understanding of what it means to be human; in more-practical terms, it affects public policy, the allocation of social resources, and the meaning of 'civil rights.'"* (Bérubé, 1997)

"Yes! Movie in class today!" This is a familiar sentiment to teachers and students alike. In addition to being entertaining, films that feature disability can be useful pedagogical tools. They can aid in diversifying the curricula in all disciplines to include disability.

Disability is an important aspect of diversity. Popular films often represent disability in ways that have more to do with understandings of normality than understandings of disability. We should note that in our analysis normality does not necessarily mean common, but rather that ideal which is propagated as normal (male, white, straight, nondisabled, etc). Learning to recognize and challenge cinematic representations of disability is one way to interrupt common stereotypes and misunderstandings held about people with disabilities.

Disabled Representation

While many films feature disability, it is important to remember that most of these films are made by nondisabled people. As such, these films are not usually about people with disabilities themselves or about how disability is an integral aspect of all of our lives. Instead, these films often feature mainstream perspectives on impairment and difference while using disability as a plot device. Mitchell and Snyder (1997) call this a *narrative prosthesis*. Disability is reduced to a tool; writers and producers disregard the lived experiences of people with disabilities and perpetuate the idea that those with disabilities are abnormal, presumably unlike nondisabled people. Thus, many films involving disability become sentimentalized accounts of overcoming disability or stories of people with disabilities living tragic lives.

What is the effect of using disability as a plot device? While some may say it simply tells an intriguing or exciting story, the use of disability also creates what Paul Darke (1998) identified as the *normality drama*. In it, the "central theme is not the impairment or the abnormality but the degree to which it can either define or validate its opposite: normality." (p. 187) In such films, the character with a disability affirms normality by making the lead nondisabled characters look like compassionate individuals or by teaching them valuable life lessons. Once the character with a disability has fulfilled her or his role, s/he is literally removed. The message sent is that disability or other differences from "normal" have no place in society and must be eliminated. This may seem far-fetched at first, so let us take a closer look.

In *Rain Man* (Guber, 1988), Tom Cruise's character, shallow playboy Charlie Babbit, represents normality. His brother Raymond Babbit, played by Dustin Hoffman, performs some of the stereotypical characteristics of the autistic savant. Throughout the film the cynical and frenetic Charlie learns to appreciate life and love his brother after road tripping with Raymond and getting to know his presumably simple ways. Raymond humanizes his brother; Charlie becomes deep and caring through this relationship. When Charlie turns this new leaf, Raymond, having fulfilled his purpose in the film, is sent back to the institution.

Viewers accept this because while they appreciate Raymond's supposed simplicity, they also fear his outbursts. They condescendingly accept him but are led to believe that people with autism or other disabilities have no place in society. The inhumanity of large institutions and the successes of school and community inclusion clearly show that this is not the case. However, audiences leave the movie thinking that institutionalization is really for Raymond's own good rather than about society's discomfort with difference. Darke (1998) explains, "a physically or mentally impaired character is represented to reinforce the illusions of normality: a normality exhibited either in a film's non-impaired characters or by the impaired character's rejection of their impaired self." (p. 184) Characters with disabilities become expendable once they have sufficiently humanized the lead character. In the end, normality is restored through either rehabilitation/normalization of the disabled character, or through the character's death or exile from the community. Examples of humanizers who die at the end of their films include Kevin in *The Mighty* (Forte, 1998), Georges in *The Eighth Day* (Josset, 1996), Jane in *The Theory of Flight* (Thompson, 1998), and Simon Birch in *Simon Birch* (Baldecchi, 1998).

Since many characters with disabilities simply serve the purpose of humanizing the other characters, the characters with disabilities often become one-dimensional and cliché. People with disabilities in films are usually objects of pity; tragic victims; humorous subjects; dangerous or malevolent criminals; monsters; or revenge-seeking malcontents (Bogdan & Biklen, 1977; Bogdan, Biklen, Shapiro & Spelkoman, 1982; Longmore, 2003; Norden, 1994). There are few alternatives to these repeated representations that marginalize characters with disabilities; thus, their marginalization seems to be the natural order of things. Following are a few examples of some of the most clichéd roles for characters with disabilities in movies.

The "sweet innocent" (Norden, 1994) is a role in which a character with a disability is considered an eternal child, tragically "special" and/or wholly innocent. Such characters often come with over-protective parents who may espouse that their adult son or daughter really has the mental age of a child. Audiences inevitably accept this in spite of the obvious fact that such characters have more years of experience living life. Examples of this role include Carla and Daniel, played by Juliette Lewis and Giovanni Ribisi in *The Other Sister* (Hoberman, 1999); Radio, played by Cuba Gooding Jr. in *Radio* (Garner, 2003); and Sam, played by Sean Penn in *i am sam* (Polstein, 2001). This character role simplifies and infantilizes people with disabilities and sets low expectations for them, denying them the rights of adulthood. Further, it perpetuates the belief that mental age is a useful concept and that intelligence can be discretely measured.

In another common theme, the presence of disability in a character represents evil or criminal intent. Consider the following disabled characters: Dr. Strangelove, James Bond's Dr. No, Richard III, Captain Ahab, and Captain Hook. All five seek revenge against the nondisabled world or their disabling agents, obsessively focusing on their impairments as tragedies that must be avenged. Norden (1994) aptly called this the "obsessive avenger." Disability is a negative marker for these characters and is represented as ugly, abnormal and immoral. The unmarked, nondisabled characters in many of these films seem ideal compared to their disabled counterparts. They often attempt to save the day by transforming, banishing or killing the villains so that disability is removed and normality is restored.

Lastly, let us explore the concept of the *super crip*, used extensively in news media stories about people with disabilities. This is the classic "heartwarming" tale about "courageous" people with disabilities who are "inspirational" in their efforts to "overcome" their disabilities against all odds. While this seems complementary and unproblematic on the surface, a critical look reveals underlying assumptions presuming the incompetence of people with disabilities. Eli Clare (1999) explains:

> A boy without hands bats .486 on his Little League team. A blind man hikes the Appalachian Trail from end to end. An adolescent girl with Down's Syndrome learns to drive and has a boyfriend...The nondisabled world is saturated with these stories: stories about gimps who engage in activities as grand as walking 2,500 miles or as mundane as learning to drive...They turn individual disabled people, who are simply leading their lives, into symbols of inspiration. (p. 2)

The *super crip* representation fails to interrupt the assumption that people with disabilities are incapable. It does not recognize the social and physical barriers imposed upon people with impairments that make them disabled. These stories ignore these barriers, accepting them and overly lauding individuals for their accomplishments. Instead of actually complimenting these individuals, *super crip* stories often reveal low expectations for people with disabilities. A high school student with Down syndrome who plays football should not be singled out; he is simply doing something that many other high school students are also doing. A blind marathon runner is not amazing because she ran a marathon "despite her handicap" and she is not " overcoming" her blindness in doing so. In fact, she ran it "with" her blindness, just as she does everything else in her life. A blind marathon runner is amazing because she ran a marathon and this is an amazing feat for anyone.

Films also tell these heartwarming tales and *super crip* stories that rely on charity and pity. Many glorify people with disabilities simply for living their lives and doing things that many others do on a daily basis. One consequence of these stories is that people with disabilities are expected to deny and try to "overcome" their disabilities.

This critique of the representation of disability in film is not intended to discourage teachers from incorporating these films into their classes. In fact, these films are useful tools for introducing disability issues to students in various departments and academic areas. If a film includes negative representations of disability, these representations should be addressed as part of discussion.

Film Directory

The study of disability is inherently interdisciplinary. Below is a directory (certainly not exhaustive) of provocative films that may illicit discussion about disability. By using these films in class, instructors can effectively introduce disability into their disciplines. In addition to teaching students how to critique film representations, instructors may also use these films to help students recognize and begin to challenge the power of ideologies that define normality by marking and excluding certain groups of people.

Our list of movies is loosely grouped according to the following disciplines: Anthropology/Language; Fine Arts; Gender/Women's Studies; History/Political Science; Humanities/English Literature; Law/Public Policy; Media Studies/Popular Culture; Medicine/Psychiatry/Psychology; Queer Studies and Other.

Anthropology/Language
Conceptions of disability vary significantly across cultures. How is disability perceived and constructed differently?

The Color of Paradise: An Iranian film about a boy who is blind and his relationship with his father and grandmother.
Karimi, M., Maghami, A., Mahabadi, M. Mohsen, S. (Producers), & Majidi, M. (Director). (1999). Iran: Varahonar Company.

Dancer in the Dark : Selma has emigrated with her son from Eastern Europe to America. Selma works day and night to save her son from the same disease she has, a disease that inevitably will make her blind. A unique film directed by Lars von Trier that deals with parental issues and acquired impairment.

> Jensen, P. (Producer), & von Trier, L. (Director). (2000). Denmark: Zentropa Entertainments.

The Eighth Day: A Belgian film about the relationship between two men, one of whom has Down syndrome. The film offers both progressive representations and also falls into the traps of the humanizer role.

> Josset, D. & Rommeluere, E. (Producers), & Van Dormael, J. (Director). (1996). Belgium: Eurimages.

Elling: A Norwegian film about two friends with conflicting personalities who move in together after living in an institution. This movie deals in a compelling and comedic way with the difficulties of rejoining society.

> Alveberg, D. (Producer), & Næss, P. (Director). (2001). Norway: Maipo Film- og TV Produksjon.

Liebe Perla (1999): A documentary about the Nazi's treatment of people with disabilities and the friendship between two women of short stature.

> Saloman, S. (Producer), & Rozen, S. (Director). (1999). Israel: Eden Productions.

Fine Arts

Some people might doubt that disability has a place in the fine arts. Yet some of the most memorable and successful artists in all mediums have experienced impairment and disability.

Frida: Frida chronicles the life Frida Kahlo shared with Diego Rivera. From her complex and enduring relationship with her mentor and husband to her illicit and controversial affair with

Leon Trotsky, to her provocative and romantic entanglements with women, Frida Kahlo was also struggling with an abusive husband, a life of wracking pain following a trolley accident, the amputation of a leg, and finally, drug and alcohol abuse that killed her at age 47.

> Amin, M et.al. (Producers), & Taymor, J. (Director). (2002). United States: Miramax Films.

King Gimp: An Academy Award winning documentary about artist Dan Keplinger, a man with cerebral palsy. This film takes a strong look at the importance of inclusive education and high expectations for all people. Dan is a successful artist, so this can and should be used in art classes.

> Hadary, H. & Whiteford, W. (Producers) & Whiteford, W. (Director). (1999). United States: Whiteford-Hadary Productions.

My Left Foot: The story of Christy Brown, who was born with cerebral palsy. He learned to paint and write with his only controllable limb: his left foot. Brown was assumed to be retarded until he proved his intelligence. This is a powerful distinction that helps question the validity and benefit of the concept of retardation.

> Heller, P. & Morrison, S. (Producers), & Sheridan, J. (Director). (1989). United States: Ferndale Films.

Gender/ Women's Studies
What are the intersections between women's studies and disability studies? Aspects to consider include sexuality, agency, and care giving roles and professions.

Children of a Lesser God: A teacher at a school for the deaf falls in love. Though the film is a romance, the story is concerned with what it means to be hearing impaired and includes powerful commentaries on signing versus speaking, a debate central to Deaf culture.

Palmer, P. & Sugarman, B. (Producers), & Haines, R. (Director). (1986). United States: Paramount Pictures.

Dance Me to My Song: An Australian film and Cannes selection written by and starring Heather Rose, a woman who had cerebral palsy and used a computer to communicate. The film explores her romantic relationships and her abusive relationship with her caregiver. This film is excellent for comparison with *The Theory of Flight (1998)*.

De Heer, R. et.al. (Producers), & De Heer, R. (Director). (1998). Australia: Vertigo.

My Flesh and Blood: The 2003 Sundance Documentary Feature Audience Award winner about a single mother of thirteen children with various impairments. The movie brings up issues of social services, women's work and inclusion.

Chaiken, J. (Producer), & Karsh, J. (Director). (2003). United States: Home Box Office (HBO).

Refrigerator Mothers: Influenced by psychologist Bruno Bettelheim during the 1950s through the 1970s, mental health and medical professionals claimed that autism was caused by mothers who were cold, distant, rejecting—unable to "bond properly." This theory has since been discounted, but its effects are still felt.

Hanley, J., Quinn, G., & Simpson, D. (Producers), & Simpson, D. (Director). (2002). United States: Kartemquin Educational Films.

The Sweet Hereafter: A heavy drama about a town coping with a tragic school bus accident. It focuses on one teenager, Nicole, an incest survivor and new wheelchair user. (See Ferri & May's (2002) "I'm a wheelchair girl now": Abjection, intersectionality, and subjectivity in Atom Egoyan's *The Sweet Hereafter*.)

Hamori, A. & Lantos, R. (Producers), & Egoyan, A. (Director). (1997). Canada: Alliance Communications Corporations.

The Theory of Flight: A romantic drama/comedy about a woman with motor neuron disease and her relationship with her nondisabled male friend. This film follows many classic tropes of the tragic and pitiable victim particularly with regard to sexuality. This film is excellent for comparison with *Dance Me to My Song* (1998).

> Thompson, D. (Producer), & Greengrass, P. (Director). (1998). United Kingdom: British Broadcasting Corporation

History/Political Science
People with disabilities are often used as anti-war propaganda. How does this affect the representation of people with disabilities?

The Best Years of Our Lives: Three American servicemen return after World War II to find their lives irrevocably changed by their military experience. One man has lost his hands and has become distant from his family as he struggles to overcome his disability. This is an early film featuring actors with disabilities.

> Goldwyn, S. (Producer). & Wyler, W. (Director). (1946). United States: Samuel Goldwyn Company.

Birdy: Two friends return from Vietnam, scarred in different ways. One has physical injuries, the other deals with mental issues that make him yearn to be a bird, something with which he has always been fascinated. This film can be used to compare the experiences of physical and mental health and/or cognitive impairments.

> Manson, D. (Producer), & Parker, A. (Director). (1984). United States: TriStar Pictures.

Born on the Fourth of July: The biography of Ron Kovic. Paralyzed in the Vietnam War, he becomes an anti-war and pro-human rights political activist after feeling betrayed by the country he fought for.

> Stone, O. (Producer & Director). (1989). United States: Ixtlan Corporation.

Coming Home: A woman whose husband is fighting in Vietnam falls in love with another man who received a paralyzing combat injury there. This is one of the first films to deal with disability and sexuality.

> Hellman, J. (Producer), & Ashby, H. (Director). (1978). United States: Jerome Hellman Productions.

The Deer Hunter: The story of three friends captured during the Vietnam War who try to deal with their haunting memories of a real game of Russian Roulette. The movie incorporates both mental illness and physical disability. This film can be used to compare the experiences of physical and mental health and/or cognitive impairments.

> Cimino, M. (Producer & Director). (1978).United States: Universal Pictures.

Forrest Gump: The film follows the extraordinary circumstances of Forrest Gump as he tells his life's tale to people waiting at a small town bus stop. This film has two main characters with disabilities: Forrest, who is presumed to be "mentally retarded"; and Lieutenant Dan, a Vietnam War veteran who is a double amputee. This film can be used to compare the representations of people with cognitive and physical impairments. The film includes many stereotypes and is ripe for critique.

> Finerman, W. et. al. (Producers), & Zemeckis, R. (Director). (1994). United States: Paramount Pictures.

Johnny Got His Gun: This powerful film explores the consequences of war through the experiences of a man rendered blind, deaf and immobile by bombing. It also brings up questions of personhood and autonomy, and issues of communication.

> Campbell, B. (Producer), & Trumbo, D. (Director). (1971). United States: World Entertainment.

King of Hearts: A British soldier in World War I tries to warn a French town about a bomb planted in the city. Unbeknownst to

him, the town has already been evacuated and the town's lively
inhabitants are actually the escaped members of the town's insane
asylum. The movie ultimately asks what madness really is in the
context of war.

> De Broca, P. & Juranville, J. (Producers), & De Broca, P.
> (Director). (1967). France: Compagnia Cinematografica
> Montoro.

Humanities/English Literature

The themes in literature are very similar to the issues of
representation in film described in the text above. What role does
the disabled character play? How is disability used in the text?
Why is it used in the text? What messages about disability are
conveyed? How is normal defined? What is assumed by the
author? How is order restored at the end of the text?

The Bell Jar: An adaptation of Sylvia Plath's autobiographical
novel. It details a young woman's summer in New York during the
1950s, her return home to New England, and her subsequent
breakdown.

> Arnold, M. (Producer) & Peerce, L. (Director).
> (1979).United States: AVCO Embassy Pictures.

Breathing Lessons: This documentary introduces Mark O'Brien, a
journalist and poet living in Berkeley, California. He gets around
in an iron lung, the result of polio as a child and a relapse 20 years
later. O'Brien comments on his life; his parents' courage and
devotion; his studies at the California Institute of Technology; his
writing; the sweetness of friendship; and his fears.

> Welsh, R. (Producer), & Erman, J. (Director). (1994).
> United States: Republic Pictures Corporation.

Charly: Based on the book *Flowers for Algernon* by Daniel
Keyes. A man labeled mentally retarded is temporarily "cured."
This is a great film for discussing the nature of intelligence and
the social construction of mental retardation.

Seligman, S. (Producer), & Nelson, R. (Director). (1968). United States: ABC Pictures Corporation.

Hamlet: There are several versions of this classic Shakespearean play in which a Danish prince seeks to avenge his father's death when his uncle murders his father, succeeds him as King, and marries the Queen. The play deals with mental illness (madness) and allows for discussions of its social construction.

Olivier, L. (Producer & Director). (1948). United Kingdom: Two Cities Films Ltd.

The Hunchback of Notre Dame: There are multiple versions of this film adaptation of Victor Hugo's story about Quasimodo, the bell ringer with a hunchback who falls in love with a "gypsy" girl.

Berman, P. (Producer), & Dieterle, W. (Director). (1939). United States: RKO Radio Pictures Inc.

Marat/Sade: The full title of the Peter Weiss play of which the film is a faithful rendition is *The Persecution and Assassination of Jean-Paul Marat as Performed by the Inmates of The Asylum of Charendon Under the Supervision of the Marquis de Sade*. The film is a fascinating and progressive historical perspective on class, mental illness and institutionalization.

Birkett, M. (Producer), & Brook, P. (Director). (1967). United Kingdom: Royal Shakespeare Company.

Mrs. Dalloway: A British film based on Virginia Woolf's novel exploring post-World War II society, mental health issues and choices/opportunities of women.

Ball, C. et. al. (Producers), & Gorris, M. (Director). (1997). United Kingdom: British Broadcasting Corporation.

Of Mice and Men: The cinematic adaptation of John Steinbeck's novel of the same name. It is important to note the obvious stereotypes of George, the slow and not-so gentle giant of this

American classic.
> Blomquist, A. (Producer), & Sinise, G. (Director).
> (1992). United States: Metro-Goldwyn-Mayer (MGM).

Richard III: There are multiple versions of Shakespeare's tragedy of the Duke of Gloucester. Richard III has a physical disability and rises to the throne of England by treachery, and brilliance, only to find that his own methods have prepared the groundwork for his downfall.
> Olivier, L. (Producer & Director). (1955). United
> Kingdom: London Film Productions.

Law/Public Policy

How is disability addressed in the law and policy, and how does the written word translate into practice? Do people with disabilities require special considerations or protections under the law? If so how might this infringe on individuals' personal rights? How has the history of institutionalization and discrimination segregated and/or isolated disabled people?

The Execution of Wanda Jean: A powerful documentary focusing on the execution of an African-American lesbian who is labeled mentally retarded. The film's center is at the intersection of race, gender, sexual orientation and disability amidst the horrific process of the death penalty.
> Abraham, N. (Producer), & Garbus, L. (Director). (2002).
> United States: Moxie Firecracker Films.

My Brother's Keeper: About a trial in Munnsville, N.Y., in which a man assumed to have a cognitive disability is accused of murdering his brother. The film, however, is ultimately about community inclusion, though many in the community speak *for* the accused.
> Berlinger, J. & Sinofsky, B. (Producers and Directors).
> (1992). United States: American Playhouse.

Philadelphia: A gay man with AIDS fights a legal battle regarding discrimination after being fired from his job.
>   Bozman, R. et. al. (Producers), & Demme, J. (Director). (1993). United States: Tristar Pictures.

Profoundly Normal: A television drama about a husband and wife couple who had met and fallen in love in the institution that had been their home for years. They deal with numerous challenges and opposition from social services when they decide to marry and raise a family.
>   Alley, K., et. al. (Producers), & Clifford, G. (Director). (2003). United States: Carlton America.

When Billy Broke His Head...and other Tales of Wonder: A documentary written by and starring Billy Golfus after having experienced a traumatic brain injury. Golfus challenges ableism and governmental bureaucracy related to social security income while highlighting issues and individuals within the disability rights movement. This film is a classic.
>   Golfus, B. & Simpson, D. (Directors). (1995). United States: Independent Television Service.

Media Studies/Popular Culture
How do satire and other subversive media differ from films that offer stigmatizing representations of disability? What would it take to represent a character with a disability in an unsentimental manner as a completely developed character who happens to have a disability. Better yet, why not hire a disabled actor to play her or him?

There's Something About Mary: Excerpts from this film can be useful in illustrating the humanizer role. Mary's brother Warren is represented as the stereotypical mentally retarded person with a thrift store jacket, high-water pants, blank stare, goofy wave, repetitive phrases and uncontrollable strength. This representation provides comic relief of the "laughing at" variety in the film. Ben Stiller, playing Ted, proves to Mary that he's a good guy by defending Warren from bullies at school. Warren is not a fully developed character; he is present to serve the purpose of humanizing Ted in Mary's (and the audience's) eyes.

Farrelly, P., Farrelly, B. et. al. (Producers), & Farrelly, P., Farrelly, B. (Directors). (1998). United States: 20th Century Fox.

50 First Dates: Henry Roth is a veterinarian living in Hawaii who enjoys the company of vacationing women. He leaves the playboy life behind after he falls for Lucy Whitmore. Lucy experiences short-term memory loss. Since she can never remember meeting him, Henry has to romance Lucy every single day and hope that she falls for him. Eventually, they develop respectful and effective ways to support her and their relationship. A good film for examining the differences between the medical and social models of disability.

Ewing, M et. al. (Producers), & Segal, P. (Director). (2004). United States: Columbia Pictures Corporation.

A Different Approach: An all-star educational film about the positive side of hiring people with disabilities. A fictional California mayors' committee sits and watches the film that an up-and-coming director (Michael Keaton) has assembled to sell companies on "hiring the handicapped." The film takes "a different approach" by combining several hilarious approaches.

Belcher, J. & Field, F. (Producers). (1978). United States.

Four Weddings and a Funeral: One of the few examples of a film in which a character with a disability is just that: a character who happens to have a disability. David Bower plays David, the deaf brother of Charles (Hugh Grant). David is deaf in real life and signs throughout the movie.

Fellner, E. et. al. (Producers), & Newell, M. (Director). (1994). Great Britain: Channel Four Films.

Freaks: Tod Browning's cult classic that was banned for many years stars actual circus performers who exact revenge on a mendacious "normate" trapeze artist.

> Browning, T. (Producer & Director). (1932). United States: Metro-Goldwyn-Mayer.

Pumpkin: The perfect sorority girl falls in love with a "mentally challenged athlete" she was coaching for charity. This movie is a campy satire of university Greek life and challenges traditional notions of disability. This is an excellent social critique, which includes an over-the-top, overprotective mom.

> Coppola, F. F. et. al. (Producers), & Abrams, A., Broder A. L. (Directors). (2002). United States: American Zoetrope.

The Station Agent: A man of short stature moves to an abandoned train depot in rural New Jersey when his friend and partner dies. Though he tries to maintain a life of solitude, he is soon entangled with an artist who is struggling with a personal tragedy and an overly friendly hot dog vendor. This is one of the few films that portrays disability without the sentimentality of common stereotypes of disability as tragedy.

> Tucker, K. et. al. (Producers), & McCarthy, T. (Director). (2003). United States: SenArt Films.

Stuck On You: In this comedy, conjoined twins from Martha's Vineyard move to Los Angeles so that one of them can pursue an acting career. The film responds to many stereotypes regarding disability and is helpful in trying to mark the fine line between laughing *with* versus laughing *at* disability. The film features many actors with disabilities.

> Farrelly, P., Farrelly, B. et. al. (Producers), & Farrelly, P., Farrelly, B. (Directors). (2003). United States: 20th Century Fox.

Medicine/Psychiatry/Psychology

Conflict exists between a medical view of disability, which locates deficits in the individual, and a social view of disability, which identifies environmental problems such as inaccessibility and prejudice at the root of disability (Linton 1998). How can this be reconciled in theory and in practice? Where does one draw the line between developing supports and finding cures? What does it really mean to strive to cure disability? How might the consumer/survivor/ex-patient movement influence treatment?

Awakenings: The true story of a group of comatose patients at an institution and their ensuing "awakening." This film raises the issue of high expectations for all people and humanity in the practice of medicine.

     Schmidt, A. et. al. (Producers), & Marshall, P. (Director). (1990). United States: Columbia Pictures Corporation.

A Beautiful Mind: The story of the meteoric rise of John Forbes Nash Jr., a math prodigy who is able to solve problems that had baffled the greatest of minds. The film incorporates his experiences with schizophrenia and his Nobel Prize.

     Kehela, K. et. al. (Producers), & Howard, R. (Director). (2001). United States: Imagine Entertainment.

Benny and Joon: A romantic comedy about a woman with mental illness, her independence, romance and family relationships. This film is an excellent tool for discussing sibling relationships and overprotectiveness, as well as the benefits and possibilities of natural supports.

     Badalato, B. (Producer), & Chechik, J. (Director). (1993). United States: Metro-Goldwyn-Mayer.

The Elephant Man: A Victorian doctor cares for a man with Proteous Syndrome. This film can be used to explore questions of humanity and diversity related to disfigurement and/or impairment. See also Tod Browning's *Freaks* (1932) and *The Hunchback of Notre Dame* (1939).

> Cornfeld, S. (Producer), & Lynch, D. (Director). (1980). Great Britain: Brooksfilms Ltd.

Girl, Interrupted: Adapted from the book by Susanna Kaysen. This movie explores women's lives at a mental hospital in the 1960s. The film can also be useful in English literature classes.

> Ryder, W. et. al. (Producers), & Mangold, J. (Director). (1999). United States: Columbia Pictures Corporation.

One Flew Over the Cuckoo's Nest: The film adaptation of Ken Kesey's classic. This is a sharp commentary on mental health, institutions and the more sordid psychiatric "therapies." The movie can also be useful in English literature classes.

> Zaentz, S. & Douglas, M. (Producers), & Forman, M. (Director). (1975). United States: Fantasy Films.

Twitch and Shout: A documentary focusing on the lives of several individuals with Tourette's Syndrome produced by a photojournalist with Tourette's. The film includes compelling discussions of social stigmatization, self advocacy, and reactions to ableism.

> Chiten, L. (Producer & Director). (1993). United States.

Queer Studies

The intersection of marked groups is a powerful place. What are the similarities and differences between ableism and heteronormativity? Where do Queer Studies and Disability Studies support each other? Where do they conflict?

And the Band Played On: The story of the discovery of the AIDS virus from the early days in 1978 when numerous San Francisco gay men began dying from unknown causes to the identification of the HIV virus.

> Spelling, A. (Producer), & Spottiswoode, R. (Director). (1993). United States: Home Box Office.

As Good As It Gets: A normality drama great for exploring the intersection of disability studies, including the consumer/survivor/ex-patient movement, and queer theory. Jack Nicholson, as Melvin, displays characteristics of obsessive-compulsive disorder, which ostensibly prevents him from leading a "normal" life. Through medication and love, Melvin is able to "cure" his disability and become normal again. (See Robert McRuer's (2003) "As Good as it Gets: Queer Theory and Critical Disability.")

Ziskin, L. et. al. (Producers), & Brooks, J. (Director). (1997). United States: TriStar Pictures.

F**k the Disabled (Keeping It Real): Based on Greg Walloch's one-man autobiographical show *White Disabled Talent*, *Keeping It Real* is part stand-up comedy, part behind-the-scenes day-in-the-life, and part dramatization of Walloch's monologues. The title of the film is based on a true story in which a female friend of Walloch asks if he is gay because he is crippled and therefore women won't sleep with him.

Thomas, L. et. al. (Producers), & Kabillio, E. (Director). (2001). United States: Mad Dog Films, Inc.

Other (Quality films that didn't quite fit in any other category)

Finding Nemo: An animated children's film that speaks back to over-protective parents. Nemo, a clown fish with a "lucky" fin, tries to escape an aquarium as his worried father and sidekick Dory (a fish with short-term memory loss) search the sea for him. High expectations, natural supports, diversity and self-confidence are additional themes.

Lasseter, J. (Producer), & Stanton, A., Unkrich, L. (Directors). (2003). United States: Pixar Animation Studios.

Flawless: A tough, conservative security guard suffers a stroke during a robbery. His recovery requires him to take voice lessons from his drag queen neighbor. The unlikely pair learns to look beyond differences and find common ground in friendship. The movie focuses on communication and interrogates the emphasis on speaking.

Machlis, N. (Producer), & Schumacher, J. (Director). (1999). United States: Tribeca Productions.

Regarding Henry: The story of a lawyer who survives a shooting. He cannot remember anything and must work to recover his speech and mobility. This film focuses on rehabilitation and family support.

Greenhut, R. (Producer), & Nichols, M. (Director). (1991). United States: Paramount Pictures.

Sound and Fury: This Academy Award-nominated documentary follows one extended family on a unique journey as two sets of parents deal with the question of getting cochlear implants for their deaf children. Two of the parents are hearing and two of the parents are Deaf. The film educates viewers about Deaf culture and raises issues around diversity, humanity, affiliation, and inclusion. It is as challenging as it is effective.

Weisberg, R. (Producer), & Aronson, J. (Director). (2000). United States: Aronson Fil Associates.

What's Eating Gilbert Grape?: This unique story of a rural family (the Grapes) avoids many of the classic tropes regarding disability. Gilbert dreams of moving away until he recognizes his strong bonds with brother Arnie who experiences unnamed cognitive differences, their two sisters, and their loving, obese mother.

Hallstrom, L. et. al. (Producers), & Hallstrom, L. (Director). (1993). United States: Paramount Pictures.

Mia Feldbaum is a graduate student earning her Master's Degree in Cultural Foundations of Education and Disability Studies at Syracuse University.

Zach Rossetti is currently pursuing a Ph.D. in Special Education and Disability Studies at Syracuse University.

References

Baldecchi, J. (Producer) & Johnson, M. (Director). (1998). *Simon Birch* [Motion Picture]. United States: Hollywood Pictures.

Bérubé, M. (1997). On the cultural representation of people with disabilities. *The Chronicle of Higher Education*. Retrieved September 21, 2004 from the World Wide Web: http://chronicle.com/prm/che-data/articles.dir/art-43.dir/issue38.dir/38b00401.htm

Bogdan, R. & Biklen, D. (1977). Handicapism. *Social Policy, 7*, 14-19.

Bogdan, R., Biklen, D., Shapiro, A., & Spelkoman, D. (1982). The disabled: Media's monster. *Social Policy, 13*, 32-35.

Clare, E. (1999). *Exile & Pride: Disability, Queerness, and Liberation*. Cambridge: South End Press.

Darke, P. (1998). Understanding cinematic representation of dis ability. In Shakespeare (Ed.). *The Disability Reader: Social Science Perspectives*. London: Continuum, 181–197.

Forte, D., Goldstein, J., Weinstein, B., Weinstein, H., (Producers), & Chelsom, P. (Director). (1998). *The Mighty* [Motion Picture]. United States: Miramax Films.

Garner, T., Scanlon, C. (Producers), & Tollin, M. (Director). (2003), *Radio* [Motion Picture]. United States: Revolution Studios.

Guber, Peter (Producer), & Levinson, B. (Director). (1988). *Rain Man* [Motion Picture]. United States: Mirage Entertainment.

Hoberman, D. (Producer), & Marshall, G. (Director). (1999). *The Other Sister* [Motion Picture]. United States: Touchstone Pictures.

Linton, S. (1998). *Claiming disability: Knowledge and identity.* New York: New York University Press.

Longmore, P. (2003). *Why I burned my book and other essays on disability.* Philadelphia: Temple University Press.

May, V. & Ferri, B. (2002). "I'm a wheelchair girl now": Abjection, intersectionality, and subjectivity in Atom Egoyan's *The Sweet Hereafter. Women's Studies Quarterly, 30*, 131-150.

McRuer, R. (2003). As good as it gets: Queer theory and critical disability. *GLQ. 9*: 1&2, 79-105.

Mitchell, D. (2002). Narrative prosthesis and the materiality of metaphor. In Snyder, Brueggemann, & Garland-Thomson (Eds.) *Disability studies: Enabling the humanities.* New York: MLA Press.

Mitchell, D. & Snyder, S. (1997). *The body and physical difference: Discourses of disability.* Ann Arbor, MI: University of Michigan Press.

Norden, M. (1994). *The cinema of isolation: A history of physical disability in the movies.* New Brunswick, NJ: Rutgers University Press.

Polstein, C., Rubin, D. (Producers), & Nelson, J. (Director). (2001). *i am sam* [Motion Picture]. United States: New Line Cinema.

Thomson, R.G. (1997). *Extraordinary bodies: Figuring physical disability in American culture and literature.* New York: Columbia University Press.

Thomson, R.G. (2002). The politics of staring: Visual rhetorics of disability in popular photography. In Snyder, Brueggemann, & Garland-Thomson (Eds.) *Disability studies: Enabling the humanities*. New York: MLA Press.

"Krazy Kripples": Using *South Park* to Talk about Disability

Julia White

Shocking, irreverent, obscene, politically incorrect and offensive are words commonly used to describe Comedy Central's animated series *South Park*. The characters have become cultural icons; the words "Oh my god, they've killed Kenny! The bastards!" have entered our cultural lexicon, and to the dismay of parents and teachers around the world, kids buy *South Park* lunchboxes, notebooks, clothing and toys. Nothing is immune to the satirical lampoon of creators Matt Stone and Trey Parker; they have produced episodes focusing on issues ranging from hate-crime legislation to international food relief efforts to stem cell research. The episodes serve as social commentary on the duplicity of government, the power of the media and the proclaimed moral superiority of fundamentalism. Furthermore, whether they realize it or not, and I suspect they do, Parker and Stone tackle disability issues with a consciousness rarely seen in film or on television. They simultaneously present and contest stereotypes of disabled people and other populations through the sometimes absurd Aristotelian plotlines (exposition, rising action, climax, falling action and resolution) to arrive at the "moral" of the episode.

South Park episodes can be used as springboards for classroom discussions of many issues in a variety of disciplines including, but not limited to, philosophy, bioethics, English/textual studies, sociology and education. Discussions that arise through such exploration—cultural critiques through satire, stereotypes of disability, group identity and the attitude of the "normate" toward disability issues—can potentially provide a different lens through which to interpret texts, or introduce students to the existence of invisible minorities. Since the introduction of two disabled characters in seasons 4 and 5, a few episodes have focused peripherally on disability, and many can be considered "crip-centric." Of particular pedagogical interest is one episode, "Krazy Kripples," which highlights themes and issues from disability studies and disability culture.

"How many able-bodied does it take to change a light bulb?"

South Park is set in the fictional community of South Park, Colorado, a suburb of Denver. The characters are themselves stereotypes: Cartman, the fat kid; Kyle, the Jewish kid; Stan, the smart kid; and Kenny, the poor kid. They are fourth graders at South Park Elementary School, and their school and town is populated with various stereotypical characters. Among them are Big Gay Al, Chef, Sheila Broflovski, Uncle Jimbo, Priest Maxi, Mr. Mackey and the owner of City Wok, who appear almost weekly. Nearly every episode has a guest "appearance" by a celebrity. Each episode, in typical sit-com fashion, begins with a problem, which launches a series of usually satiric events that often become fantastic, carnivalesque or absurd, and usually ends with a moralizing speech about the resolved conflict. In the fourth and fifth seasons, two characters are introduced who take *South Park* to a new and exciting level in American comedy television. Timmy, introduced in season 4, uses a power wheelchair and communicates by saying only his name: "Timmah!" Still, everyone understands him. Jimmy, introduced in season 5, uses crutches, has a speech disorder and aspires to be a stand-up, "handi-capable" comedian. Their addition to the cast gives Parker and Stone yet another realm of society to lampoon and allows them to delve into disability culture while simultaneously critiquing able-bodied stereotypes about disability and making us laugh uproariously. As Hart (2002) states, "*South Park* is really making fun of us—both the people who recognize the ignorance-based stereotypes that humanity has cultivated, and the people who buy into those stereotypes."

In studying media portrayals of people with disabilities, Biklen and Bogdan (1977) find that the following representations are most common: they are victorious over challenges, inspirations to able-bodied normates (e.g., the blind man who climbs a mountain), carrying chips on their shoulders, angry or bitter because of their disabilities or sinister or evil (e.g., Richard III or Captain Hook). The characters and plotlines in "Krazy Kripples" explore many of these stereotypes, which are often all embodied in the same character. Disabled characters are often portrayed as jokesters, jesters or butts of jokes. "Krazy Kripples," in fact, opens with Jimmy's appearance onstage for his comedy act. However, there is only one kid (Butters) in the audience because the whole town has gone to hear Christopher Reeve speak about stem cell research. Jokes uttered by the disabled characters appear throughout this episode, serving both to impress and placate the audience thereby reifying stereotypes. In "Cripple Fight," a previous episode in which he was introduced, Jimmy tells the following joke: "I just flew into South Park. Boy, are my crutches tired." Similarly, in this episode, Christopher Reeve opens his speech with a variation of Jimmy's joke: "I just flew into South Park. Used to be I didn't need an airplane." The audience responds with "ahhs" and applause. However, laugher and jokes are also used to reinforce Jimmy and Timmy's burgeoning recognition of and entrance into disability culture. Jokes served to transgress and subvert stereotypes about disability and turn them onto the "normate," the able-bodied, as when Jimmy and Timmy decide to form a club that accepts as members only those who were "crippled from birth." In letting the other boys know they may not join this club, Jimmy uses well-known jokes previously applied to disability and other groups: "Hey Timmy. How many able-bodied people does it take to screw in a

light bulb? One. [Timmy and Jimmy begin to laugh.] You know
what you call an able-bodied guy on the doorstep? Whatever his
name is. [They walk away laughing]."

Christopher Reeve, who comes to South Park to talk about
stem cell research, is characterized at some point in the episode by
all the stereotypical representations of disability: jokester,
inspiration, super-crip and evil. Reeve, in a not-so-subtle nod to
the controversy surrounding him in the disability community, is
first presented as the super-crip, an inspiration. Reeve focuses on
curing his disability at any cost, and in doing so he excludes and
dismisses any focus on the daily lives of disabled people, which
has made him anathema for many in the disability community.
When Jimmy asks why everyone has gone to see Reeve and did
not come to his comedy show, Butters tells him, "because he got
crippled, but now he can move his finger. He is an inspiration to
us all." In her introduction, the Mayor states, "And so without
further ado, here's the most courageous, most amazing man on the
planet, Christopher Reeve." To hit us over the head with the
stereotype hammer, at various points through the episode,
characters state: "Oh, what a fighter." "That brave, brave man."
"He's an inspiration to us all."

But "super-crip" takes on a different meaning in this
episode, one loaded with popular culture irony. Reeve goes on
Larry King Live to demonstrate how stem cells help him, and how
he uses stem cells. Reeve takes a fetus, breaks its neck open, and
slurps from the back of its neck. Reeve becomes more and more
maniacal and obsessed with the power he gets from the stem cells,
morphing into the stereotype of disability as evil. This particular
scene would be useful in discussions surrounding the politics,
ethics, and controversy surrounding stem cell research. The way
that Reeve uses the fetuses, while exaggerated and unrealistic,
effectively captures the stereotypical perception that the American
public has about stem cell research. This parallel plot episode
then moves into a parody of *Superman*, with Gene Hackman
coming to South Park to campaign against stem cell research,
thwarting Reeve's efforts to find a cure for his disability. Angry

because he lives in a wheelchair and is being pushed around by others, Reeve becomes increasingly evil and forms a Legion of Doom to stop "Hack-Man." At the end of the episode, Reeve ends up in Lex Luthor's Phantom Zone, promising revenge.

"Are they crippled from birth or are they cripple wannabes?"

The other plot in this episode moves away from a critique of media representations of the disabled and deals with a sometimes divisive issue in the disability community—disabled from birth versus acquired disability later in life—and the identity politics that surround this issue. Early in the episode, as Jimmy confronts his friends about their failure to attend his comedy show, the medical model of disability is presented in a rather subversive way that viewers might easily miss, a subtly brilliant way. While Jimmy calls his friends on not attending his comedy show, Reeve's speech to the crowd, barely audible, but purposefully placed in the pauses in the kids' conversation, illustrates why Reeve is so controversial (Reeve's speech is in italics):

> Jimmy: Say, fellas! Thanks a lot for goin' to my ... c-comedy show!
> *["It is a proven fact that stem-cell research"]*
> Cartman: We didn't go to your comedy show.
> Jimmy: I know that, I was being f-f-f-fa...cetious!
> *["can add many years to the lives of people who have been disabled by accidents"]*
> Stan: Look, dude. Christopher Reeve, dude.
> *["or other ways."]*

Jimmy recognizes the emphasis that Reeve puts on acquired disability and also how his agenda detracts from an understanding of the lives and social situations of people born with disabilities: "Why is a celebrity who became crippled more important than us that were born that way, very much." This scene is rich in topics for classroom discussion around the social, economic, and political opportunities, or lack thereof, or people with disabilities and other marginalized groups.

Jimmy and Timmy decide to start a club ("... not only do you have to be c-c-crippled, but you have to have been *born* that way. Do you know what that means? No butthole Superman asswipe Christopher Reeve!"). They flat out tell the boys that they cannot be members and proceed to tell the able-bodied jokes about them. They take their T-shirt design to Mr. McGillicuddy to have it printed; their design says, "The Crips." Mr. McGillicuddy tells them that there already is a group called "The Crips" and that they would not like the boys to use their name. Jimmy immediately wants to know about them, asking, "Are they crippled from birth or are they cripple wannabes like Christopher Reeve?" He then excitedly states to Timmy, "All this time there was a group for truly crippled people like ourselves, and we didn't know it." They venture off to try to connect with them and end up becoming members of the Crips gang (after they inadvertently kill 13 Bloods). In the preliminary "interview" with the Crips gang, the issue of disabled at birth verses acquired disability is further explored:

> Jimmy: We just have one question before we join your c-club. Do you think it's better to be *born* a Crip, or to become a Crip later by accident?
> Braided Crip: The only Crips is born Crips, dawg.
> Tall Crip: Yeah, you can't become a Crip by accident, fool!
> Jimmy: I agree. I mean, it's like *[enunciates]* "come on"! Why do these people who become crippled later in life think they're such great pot-potatuhs?

Jimmy and Timmy become part of this gang, and begin identifying themselves with the gang. More importantly, they recognize they are part of a minority group and begin identifying themselves as such; they wear the group's colors and appropriate its language and cultural expressions. In turn, they are fully accepted by the Crips, who give them the monikers "Roller" and

"Four Legs." Jimmy proclaims, "Timmy, I have a feeling that this is the start of something b-b-b-b...b-b-brilliant." *South Park* also examines the intersection of race and disability through a critique of racial and disabled (non)presence in both the town of South Park, Colorado, and in wider suburban America, as Jimmy ponders, "That's an amm-mmazing coincidence. I mean, there's not one crippled colored person in South Park."

Jimmy and Timmy, through a series of outlandish events leading to the moralizing end of this cautionary tale, finally realize that they "should have never started a gang for people crippled from birth. Now they're at war with the people who are crippled from an accident. Boy were we wrong." The boys arrange a lock-in at the recreation center to broker a truce, but the Bloods and the Crips pull their weapons on each other. To diffuse the situation, Jimmy tells them that he was wrong for "player-hatin' Christopher Butthole Reeve," and then he utters his catch phrase, "Come on." At that point, the Crips and the Bloods resolve their differences. On its face, "Come on" is an absurd utterance, but it also underscores the absurdity of the position of both the rival gangs and the birth-versus-acquired camps. In typical *South Park* style, the conflict is resolved quickly through a moralizing speech, and while Christopher Reeve is sailing through space, the Crips and Bloods play basketball together, get high and perform a Fat Albert-esque song ("Friendly Thugs").

In commenting on the position of the able-bodied "normate" in disability (and Black urban) culture, the four main characters—Stan, Kyle, Cartman, and Kenny—appear only three short times in this episode. They literally walk through the frame, each time stating a variation of "I think we'd better stay out of this one." Mr. McGillicuddy and Professor Chaos (a member of the Legion of Doom) also express their desire to "stay out of this one." Mitchell (2002) argues that disabled characters are often used as metaphor or a "narrative prosthesis" in a text, but in this episode, it is the normate who is the metaphor, who expresses the stereotypical understanding of disability portrayals in media, and who distances himself from something he thinks is beyond his ken.

"You haven't seen the last of me, Hack Man! I will be back!!"

Initially, it appears that Jimmy and Timmy have resolved the conflict between the Crips and the Bloods, paralleling their own acceptance of the acquired-disability camp, However, the last lines of the episode—Reeves affirming, "I will be back!" and the boys' final expression that they are glad they "stayed out of this one"—signal both that the issues surrounding representations of disability and disability (and identity) politics are not going away, and that the continued avoidance of these issues by the able-bodied might not be possible.

An informed reading of the inherent satirical content of *South Park* can assist the reader (or viewer) in critiquing other texts of popular culture, including Hollywood representations of disability. An awareness of how media represents disability, how this representation influences the understandings and attitudes of the able-bodied "normate," and how those of us who interact with texts can question those understandings and attitudes will perhaps lead to the possibility of becoming engaged in disability (and other minority group) issues and in the broader social structures that in fact make these issues at all.

Julia White is a doctoral candidate in the Special Education and Disability Studies programs at Syracuse University.

References

Biklen, D. & Bogdan, R. (1977). Media portrayals of disabled persons. *International Books for Children Bulletin, 8,* 4-7.

Hart, M. (2002, October 25). "South Park," in the tradition of Chaucer and Shakespeare. *The Chronicle of Higher Education, 49*(9), B.5.

Mitchell, D. (2002). Narrative prosthesis and the materiality of metaphor. In S. Snyder, B. Brueggemann & R.G. Thomson (Eds.). *Disability Studies: Enabling the Humanities.* New York: Modern Language Association Press.

Stone, M. & Parker, T. (Writers and Directors). (2003, March 26). Krazy kripples [Television series episode] In F. Agnone (Producer), *South Park.* Los Angeles: Comedy Central. Retrieved (20 February 2004) from the World Wide Web: http://www.twiztv.com/scripts/southpark/southpark702.htm

Stone, M. & Parker, T. (Writers and Directors). (2001, June 27). Cripple Fight [Television series episode] In F. Agnone (Producer), *South Park.* Los Angeles: Comedy Central. Retrieved 20 February 2004 from the World Wide Web: http://www.spscriptorium.com/Season5/E503script.htm.

Teaching For Social Change

Kathy Kniepmann

People with disabilities are increasingly featured in films, fiction and other media. They are often presented as pitiful, needy and generally unattractive, but infrequently portrayed as interesting, realistic and complex individuals. Many images reflect social biases and present restricted life possibilities. However, films and literature have the potential to expand collective social horizons in ways that promote respect, understanding and change. Critical analysis of disability portrayals in film and literature can enhance awareness to promote dialogue and dissent for social change, personal dignity and inclusive communities.

With this in mind, I developed an undergraduate course to help students understand social participation and disability through the exploration of film and literature. The course, "Images of disability: Portrayal in film & literature," is an elective for undergraduates from any field of study. Many of the course participants are pursuing careers in health, law or business and feel that this information will help in their future professions. Others are interested because they have family or friends with disabilities.

The course description states: This course will critically examine portrayal of persons with disabilities in literature and film, exploring how those images reflect or shape/reform impressions of the general public. Perspectives from social science, health care, communications and other fields will provide frameworks for discussion. Literature will include fiction, biography and autobiography in books, essays, drama, poetry and short stories. Popular films will be reviewed during the semester. We will also examine images in newspapers, magazines and advertising.

A growing number of Americans (more than 1 in 7) have disabilities, and many of them experience extensive misunderstanding and stigma. By exploring and analyzing fictional and biographical, or autobiographical, messages about disability experience, students will improve their critical thinking and develop increased disability awareness. This may enable them to move beyond stereotypes and increase their comfort level and sensitivity. Students interested in health care and human service careers, politics, business, or law will build better understanding and appreciate advocacy issues. Anyone, regardless of academic major or career goals, can become a better informed citizen with more appreciation of the diversity of human experience through participation in this course.

Course Content and Educational Strategies

Popular films and documentaries are powerful catalysts for class discussions and debates. In this course, I use films more than literature, since mass media have stronger influence on American culture (Bandura, 2001). Several short stories and excerpts from novels are discussed throughout the semester as well. Critical/analytical readings from social sciences, public health, literary critiques, and media studies help frame our discussions. Students are also encouraged to bring articles from their own academic fields related to course topics.

A major goal is to promote a richer awareness of human diversity and of disability as a social construction. For many students, it is difficult to let go of the medical model that focuses on deficits and "fixing" individuals. Several students express concern about diagnoses, etiology, symptoms, treatment options and prognoses, especially at the start of the course. To facilitate open discussion and expansive thinking, I encourage students to abide by the following guidelines:

They must understand that the course is a learning community. All participants can learn from each other. Sharing a range of ideas is vital for the learning process.

Students should formulate their opinions about disabilities, media, and society and then examine how they developed these ideas. All students are encouraged to question each other and to disagree, but they should question respectfully and tolerate different opinions.

Students should ponder these questions for each film, writing or other media analyzed in the course: What are their immediate responses to the films and/or literature? What are their feelings, opinions and ideas about possible social consequences and implications of the images? How do they think they might react if they had similar disabilities to those of the characters portrayed (or if they were family members)? How might this portrayal influence the general public? If they think the portrayal is harmful, what should be done? What can *they* do? How can *they* make a difference?

Early in the semester I present two key concepts from social cognitive theory (Bandura, 1986 & 2001): In *reciprocal determinism*, the environment influences individuals or groups and, in turn, allows people to shape their environments. The concept of *modeling* suggests that people can learn vicariously from others, particularly if models seem familiar or share similar characteristics. I then ask students for childhood recollections of characters with disabilities from television, movies or books. I encourage them to think about how these images have influenced their impressions of living with a disability and whether they can identify any positive role models who have disabilities. When asked what I mean by disability, I propose that we can use a variety of concepts in its definition.

Most students are surprised at the paucity of positive images they can recall. They realize that these images generate pity, fear, or occasionally, admiration for "heroes who overcame their disabilities." When I push them to consider what effects these images might have on children who have disabilities, many students express concern about a sense of invisibility or "not counting." Throughout the semester, I suggest trying to shift our focus from disabled people as "people with problems." I encourage students to examine social reactions and behaviors as well as environmental barriers and resources (or often lack thereof).

As part of the course, we read H. G. Wells' short story "The country of the blind" (1913) and Kenneth Jernigan's speech *Blindness: Is literature against us?* (1999). We also watch *The miracle worker* (Penn, A., 1962), *The color of paradise* (Majidi, M., 1999) and *At first sight* (Winkler, I., 1999). In his speech, Jernigan identifies nine bewildering and dehumanizing themes for the portrayal of the blind in literature from ancient Greece to modern times. He finds only a few modern writers who are beginning to transcend these limited themes to present fuller, richer characters. Students sometimes summarily dismiss Jernigan as bitter and over-reactive, while his critical perspectives push others to reexamine their own attitudes and consider literature and portrayal of persons with disabilities in new ways.

In "The country of the blind," a man named Nunez falls from a mountain in Ecuador and is lost. Wandering along, he finds an isolated village in a beautiful valley. When he notices houses with splotchy painting and no windows, he thinks to himself that they must be blind. Nunez subsequently learns that they are, in fact, all blind and he resolves to be their savior. But the villagers, who have been blind for 14 generations, have designed an environment and had formulated procedures that enabled them to live very well without sight. In fact, they believe that Nunez has the problem. The villagers are perplexed by his stumbling and his use of "meaningless words" like vision, sight and blindness. Nunez wants to fix for them things they do not perceive as problems. They, in turn, find Nunez to be a dysfunctional misfit.

"The country of the blind" is written so compellingly that students sometimes want to know what, exactly, caused the villagers to lose their vision and why they had not sought a cure. Others recognize how well the villagers are able to function in a setting that they designed for themselves, without barriers. It is difficult for me to maintain my composure when some students express anger at "stubborn villagers who do not want to see, and their lack of gratitude for Nunez's attempts to help them." I ask the students whether they would all want to be fixed if they were living happily in that village. By acknowledging and exploring a range of reactions, I set the stage for students to consider new viewpoints. I emphasize that we can challenge each other, but that we need to listen, withhold judgment and maintain respect for new ideas.

Documentaries such as *Sound and fury* (Weisberg R., 2000) and *Max & the magic pill* (KMOV-TV, 1995) give students an insider perspective of people with disabilities and of how environmental factors can become barriers. In one class, a student exclaimed with surprise: "It's not just the symptoms; there are challenges all around." After presenting information about the prevalence of disabilities, I ask students what they might do so people with disabilities will not face so many barriers. In our discussions, students begin to recognize that barriers are not only architectural; they are also attitudes, policies and more. I need not preach a social model of disability or the need for activism; students discovered it on their own.

To add to the human aspect of understanding disability, I invite several guest speakers to share stories about living with disabilities, and perspectives on media portrayals. Students generally feel this is a powerful contribution to their growing knowledge. For some, it is their first opportunity to ask questions about living with a disability or to hear about the subject firsthand. This helps students think differently about relatives, friends or acquaintances with disabilities. One guest speaker shattered assumptions of depression or shame by emphasizing that he enjoyed a full life with his disability, not in spite of it.

Rather than set forth an "absolute definition" of disability, I ask students to formulate their own definitions based on what they read, hear, see and believe. We discuss implications of various definitions. Some students are more insistent about wanting to find the right definition, while others are comfortable examining concepts and debating the reasons for definitions in various contexts (political, social, economic, medical, service eligibility...). Rather than impose perspectives or declare absolutes, I push them to explore implications and to examine incidents or messages from multiple academic perspectives. Students struggle to find images of disability from the media that they would recommend as positive role models.

Student feedback from the course emphasizes that they learn to examine messages more critically, formulate strategies for advocacy and social change and look beyond symptoms or conditions. A particularly compelling realization for many students is that societal factors, rather than individual difference, present major barriers for participation and quality of life.

Following are a few revelations from past students:

One student was embarrassed to admit that she previously thought nursing homes were compassionate: a nice place for people who couldn't take care of themselves. She came to realize how much they dehumanize and how important it is to have more community services.

"I realized that it's possible to enjoy life with a disability, but often other people and building designs make it much harder than it has to be."

"Pity is not nice. It doesn't help; it belittles."

"This course raises so many challenging questions and got me to reexamine stories, films and magazine messages, to look beyond surface and stereotypes."

"In other courses I've learned a lot of definitions, equations and details that I'll forget or that may be outdated soon. Here, I learned valuable perspectives that I'll carry for a lifetime."

"I realized that my parents' home is not wheelchair accessible nor are most homes. If I need to use a wheelchair in the future, I'd be stuck. I'm going to lobby for more accessible housing."

Many students decried the staggeringly high unemployment rates for people with disabilities. They looked for ways to address that politically, in future workplaces and through volunteering with advocacy organizations.

Several pre-law students who took the course say they plan to do disability rights law or volunteer for advocacy groups such as Independent Living Centers. Graduates who took the course often stay in touch about messages they subsequently share with colleagues in medicine, business and social work, or with law-school classmates and faculty about the need to put people before symptoms.

These students are pushing to look beyond stereotypes or assumptions about disabilities, which is evidence that the course fulfills its objectives. Perspectives have been forever changed and former students are motivated to educate others. Perhaps this new understanding will become infectious and help move society past the negative images perpetuated by the media and toward a new kind of acceptance of people with disabilities as simply people.

Kathy Kniepmann is an Occupational Therapist and Health Educator at Washington University School of Medicine in St. Louis.

References

Bandura A. (1986). *Social foundations of thought and action: A social cognitive theory.* Upper Saddle River, NJ: Prentice Hall.

Bandura, A. (2001). Social cognitive theory of mass communication. In J. Bryant & D. Zillman (Eds.) *Media effects: Advances in theory and research.* (2nd ed., 121-153) Hillsdale, NJ: Lawrence Erlbaum. Retrieved July 12, 2004 from the World Wide Web: http://www.emory.edu/EDUCATION/mfp/BanMassCom.pdf

Jernigan, K. (1999). *Blindness: Is literature against us?* National Federation for the Blind. Retrieved July 10, 2004 from the World Wide Web: http://www.blind.net/bpba1974.htm

KMOV-TV, Channel 4 (Producer). (1995). *Max & the magic pill* [Motion picture]. US: ParaQuad.

Majidi, M. (Director). (1999). *The color of paradise* [Motion picture]. Iran: Sony Picture Classics.

Penn, A. (Director). (1962). *The miracle worker* [Motion picture]. United States: MGM/UA.

Weisberg R. (Producer). (2000). *Sound and fury.* US: Aronson Film Associates, Inc.

Wells, H.G. (1913). "The country of the blind." Full text retrieved July 10, 2004 from the World Wide Web: http://www.litrix.com/cblind/cblin001.htm

Winkler, I. (Director). (1999). *At first sight* [Motion picture]. United States: MGM.

II.
Designing Instruction for Everyone

Nothing Special: Becoming a Good Teacher for All

Zach Rossetti
Christy Ashby

> *Nature, after all, does not dictate which qualities will*
> *correlate with cultural achievement. It is for us to decide*
> *which aptitudes- which skills and knowledge, talents and*
> *abilities, cognitive and affective traits- are valuable and*
> *which ones are not...Maybe smartness is not an abstract,*
> *universal entity; maybe it depends on the contexts we*
> *construct (Hayman, p. 21-23).*

Introduction

Robert Hayman's quote proposes that intelligence, and how we think of it, is culturally constructed. While it is commonly believed that intelligence and competence are fixed entities that can be measured and categorized, that is in fact, not the case. Competence instead, is highly dependent on the "contexts we construct," the opportunities we create for smartness to emerge and for understanding to be demonstrated. Once we understand the importance of context in the construction of intelligence, our role as educators becomes much more complex. We are not just there to pass on information and test our students. It is our responsibility to create settings where our students, *all of them*, can successfully participate and show what they know. This includes those students traditionally constructed as being outside the ranks of the college bound. It is important to note that this does not mean lowering standards so that all can achieve. Rather, we need to be mindful of the diversity present in our classrooms and create lessons and communities that are supportive of and welcoming to all.

One might ask why should I care about disability in the classroom? How is this going to help me facilitate a recitation section for a political science class or teach a biology lab? We hope that this article will help reconceptualize disability, not as an abstract category that shows up in special education texts, but as an element of diversity that relates to all of us. Traditional conceptions of disability have been based in a deficit-driven, medical model, where the goal is to identify all of the things that are wrong with the person. This often leads to exclusion from opportunity based on limited expectations. We will address this model and its shortcomings for creating classrooms that embrace diversity. Then we will introduce a different way of conceptualizing difference, the social model. This understanding of disability locates the problems in the disabling environment rather than within the individual. By including several of our own experiences we will illustrate these different schools of thought and move on to a consideration of classroom practices that support the inclusion of a wide range of students.

Rethinking Disability

In order to reconceptualize university classrooms to be more welcoming and supportive of a diverse student population, we have to consider the ways in which disability is understood and the meaning of disability is constructed. It may be helpful here to distinguish between impairment and disability. Impairment is a medical condition, an anatomical or functional difference, which may or may not result in disability. We understand disability as a social construction – a diverse category based on the social ramifications of difference. These effects may include loss of opportunity and discrimination that are sometimes thought of as the natural consequences of impairment.

To illustrate this distinction we turn to the construction of Down syndrome. The physical experience of Down syndrome is the result of a genotypic difference on the 21st chromosome. There is, therefore, an anatomical or functional difference in the person's genetic structure. However, the manifestation of that genetic difference is highly variable. Chris Kliewer (1998) explains: "Though these genetic and physical differences are a reality outside and apart from our interpretive processes, it is the meaning we attach to the differences, the cultural constructions, that turn them into the *ones that matter* when establishing an understanding of Down syndrome." (p. 17) Unfortunately, Down syndrome has been socially constructed to mean mental retardation, inability and/or a childlike status. For example, most textbooks on special education use a picture of a person with Down syndrome to introduce their chapter on Mental Retardation (Hardman et al, p. 92; Heward, 2000; p. 201 & Heward, 2003, p. 196). There is the assumption that Down syndrome can never mean anything other than mental retardation, when in fact the outcomes for individuals with Down syndrome are much more variable. This has dangerous consequences for a person so labeled. If we inherently assume that someone with such a genetic difference will never be able to succeed academically, we will be less likely to provide them with enriching curriculum and access to academic opportunities. We will place limits on their participation and on our own responsibility to teach them strong content and support them to show us what they know.

The medical model of disability focuses on the problems of the individual. On the surface that seems understandable as individualized education is recognized as being essential to progress in school. Unfortunately, this also constructs disability as something that resides within the individual. The person deviates from societal standards of normality in such a way as to require a specialized, and often separate, education. Teachers and researchers look for what is missing or deficient in the individual that is preventing her or him from succeeding in school.

Christy, one of the authors, is a for   special education

teacher and critical of her training. She remembers:

> I thought I would become a special education teacher and I
> would unlock the mysteries hiding inside the troubled
> minds and bodies of these "disadvantaged children." I took
> courses in behavioral analysis and diagnostic prescriptive
> teaching. I gave standardized assessments and charted
> progress. I saw my role as fixing the things that were
> broken or lacking in each person. I had completely bought
> into the medical model approach to education. I can
> remember actually saying that I should teach the students
> who needed me the most, the toughest kids, the ones no
> one else wanted to teach. I focused all of my attention on
> the individual student without ever considering the
> educational and social structures that had crafted that
> student's educational path.

> Later, I began to challenge the constructs of 'regular' and
> 'special,' 'normal' and 'abnormal.' I started questioning the
> two highly segregated systems of education: one for the
> regular kids and one for the kids who do not fit into
> societal constructions of "normal." Even in supposedly
> inclusive settings there is often the underlying assumption
> that some students inherently belong in the classroom and
> others have to be "included." While the distinction may
> seem subtle, the implications are not. How is it that certain
> students are perceived as so fundamentally different from
> their peers? I began to question the ways in which our
> ideas about disability are constructed and perpetuated
> through the system of education and the popular culture at
> large.

Questions such as these lead us to an understanding of the
social construction of disability and the role of context in creating
disability. The social model of disability suggests that disability is
not individual deficit but one way of understanding difference
amidst narrow definitions of normal. An individual may

experience an impairment, but this is not inherently negative. Further, it is not a disability until interacting with inaccessibility and ableism. In this way, difficulties in school must be considered from a broader environmental context. Rather than asking what the student needs to change to succeed in the classroom (or stating that certain students do not belong in our classrooms), the social model asks, "What needs to change about the classroom and the teaching to make learning happen for this student, to allow the student to show all that she or he knows?" This has major implications, not only for elementary and secondary classrooms, but for university courses as well.

We most likely all have had and most definitely will have students with disability labels in our classes. Additionally, as this article suggests, disability is not the clearly defined and essentialized identity that history has claimed it to be. All of the students that will make up our classes have unique personalities, learning styles and strengths and weaknesses regardless of any label. We will now share some of the quality educational practices that can be used to support all students to be successful learners and citizens.

Disability in the University

Many teaching assistants may feel totally unfamiliar with learning differences. They may feel that they have no experience with disability and may be unsure what to do if they have a student in their classroom that identifies as disabled. So, where to start?

Presuming the competence of all students is so important as a teaching assistant. It is often too easy to develop favorites and perceptions of who is smart in a class based on who performs in a way that matches how we are currently teaching and measuring success. This only means that in the current context, certain students are performing well. Remember the Hayman quote that we opened with? Conceptions of competence change drastically when we presume that all students are smart and that it is up to us to develop ways of supporting all students to show us what they know.

Zach, one of the authors, brings a personal perspective to the importance of presuming competence:

> I am the oldest of six children in my family. I have three brothers and two sisters. My brother Todd, in addition to being extremely outgoing, wanting to be a poet, and suffering (until recently) as a lifelong Boston Red Sox fan, has cerebral palsy. Having cerebral palsy means lots of different things to lots of different people. In Todd's case, it means that he does not speak words, gets around in a wheelchair, and does daily tasks with assistance. I disclose that information only to establish the framework of this story. While having cerebral palsy is an important part of his personality, it is by no means the only part, and is not considered a tragedy.
>
> The most difficult part of being Todd's older brother had nothing to do with him. It was witnessing the ways that he was treated in schools. When he was five, adults in his first school segregated him in his own room down the administrative hall on the other side of the gym from the classrooms. That school's principal said something to the effect of, "If God came down right now and asked Todd what one plus one was, he couldn't give the answer, so he has no place in my classes." We moved shortly after that. While Todd was "in" many of his classes in this new, supposedly more inclusive school district, he most definitely was not "with" his classmates. An aide glued to his side throughout his days, limited his interaction with classmates and potential friends. He was not tested or graded in high school. He did not use any method of communication in school other than his body language and expressions, and the high school did not commit to using various communication boards or typing on a voice output computer. Since he is often very happy and smiles a lot, he was treated like a small child and as the school mascot.

Todd missed out on a lot at school: academics, goofing around in the halls with classmates, and the anticipation and letdown of proms.

While this is an example from high school, the point is that Todd's educational successes were never based on what he could do, but on what he did--without the high expectations and supports to show all that he knew. Because he did not speak, teachers assumed he had nothing to say. Because he drooled and got around in a wheelchair, teachers saw him as "special" and treated him in very different ways than his classmates and peers. They may have thought that they were helping, but their views of disability enabled them to treat Todd disrespectfully with dire educational and social consequences. In other words, Todd was active and capable when people thought he was smart, asked him questions, and let him type to communicate. He was constructed as incompetent at school when people assumed he was retarded, segregated him and did not support his communication. Thus, the idea of disability was more a product of the environment and people's reactions to him than anything inherent in Todd's personality, body and way of doing things.

Even if we presume competence, we still might feel unsure about how to create an inclusive classroom. Where can we go for information to help us on our journey? It is crucial to use "professional literature" with caution. Be wary of any book written *about* people with disabilities that does not include the voices of people with disabilities. When looking for information about supporting a particular student, ask the person directly. If she does not wish to talk about her situation, look for first person narratives and personal accounts of disability that can counterbalance the clinical viewpoint. Returning to the earlier example of Down syndrome, we might read in the clinical literature that all students with Down syndrome lack mathematical and higher reasoning skills. How does that information help us to create classroom contexts that support learning? Wouldn't it be much more helpful and respectful to learn about someone's specific learning style, their strengths and the areas in which they can offer and will require support?

When we consider the ways we structure our classrooms and construct our lessons, we need to recognize that not all students access information in the same way. Typical university classrooms cater to students with verbal-linguistic strengths. While these are important skills and ways of learning that reflect societal and professional standards, it is just as important to recognize that not all students learn best or show all that they know through verbal-linguistic means. Utilizing a multiple intelligences approach (Gardner, 1983) to design instruction provides opportunities for active engagement in the classroom by all students. In addition, differentiating instruction (Tomlinson, 1999) means structuring lessons and assignments to allow a variety of learners to participate together and show us what they know in ways that best suit each of their learning styles.

Zach recently taught two undergraduate discussion sections of an inclusive elementary education course. He remembers:

> One student consistently turned in sloppy written work. At first, I thought she was not doing the required reading and I assumed she did not care about the course. A few weeks later, during oral presentations on topics the students chose, she gave the most thoughtful and compelling presentation of both sections. Had we not included this assignment, I would have misjudged this student's competence and the class would have missed out on a wonderful learning experience.

Try to mix up the lectures, tests, and papers with discussions, small group activities, paired work, debates, presentations, portfolios, collages, demonstrations, posters, charts, videos, visual representations of formulas and ideas and anything else you can think of. Have students lead sections of classes. Ask students how they want to present their work. Go beyond standard practices. The results will be surprising.

Allowing sufficient wait time, an aspect of universal

design, is another crucial element of inclusive pedagogy. To illustrate this point, we return to personal experience. Christy observed a student with the label of autism for a research project:

> This person types to communicate, thus requiring longer than most students to compose a response. He was struggling because by the time he had drafted a response to each question posed by the instructor, the conversation had moved on to another topic and he was now several minutes behind in the lesson. He never had an opportunity to show what he knew. Contrast this with an observation in another setting. I witnessed an instructor pose a question to the class and then allow time for the students to process what was asked. The instructor then acknowledged Sam saying, "I see that Sam has something he wants to add." The instructor then waited for Sam to finish his response so that it could be shared aloud before moving on. Another alternative would be to acknowledge the student and then say to her or him, "I see that you have something to say. I am going to hear Carla's response and then I will come back to you."

Classrooms that truly embrace diversity inherently convey to all students that they belong as they are. It is crucial to recognize that disability is indeed an important aspect of diversity. Too often diversity is framed along race and gender identities. While these are obviously imperative, this conception often fails to include class, culture, sexual orientation and dis/ability identities, which are important aspects of all of our lives. Employing culturally relevant teaching (Ladson-Billings, 1994) allows us to address, value and build upon the lived experiences of all of our students. When facilitating discussions and sharing examples in class, we must be sure to address the variety of experiences of all of our students. We can and should teach our students to critique media representations and literature that embraces oppressive norms as the natural order of things. When choosing books, films and video clips to use in our classrooms, we should include representations that share a larger array of lived experiences. In short, we can create a space that embraces all of the differences in the class community.

For example, let's say we are teaching a lesson on non-violent resistance as a force for social change. We might think of the civil rights movement in the United States or the work of Gandhi in India. Within the disability rights movement there are many examples that could be drawn on as well. In the 1980s many individuals who use wheelchairs and their allies formed the activist group ADAPT (American Disabled for Accessible Public Transit) and blockaded bus stops, prohibiting bus lines from running. These demonstrations helped bring about greater accessibility in public transportation. Another excellent example is the 1988 Gallaudet University strike. Students of this university for deaf and hard of hearing students seized control of the campus after a hearing person was appointed to the position of President. After a week of protests with the rallying slogan, "Deaf President Now," the hearing President stepped down and a new Deaf President was appointed to the post (Shapiro, 1993).

It is important to remember that all of the principles and strategies just described are not *specialized* techniques for teaching the disabled. Instead, they are elements of good teaching for *all* students. As the title of this essay implies, there is nothing special about good teaching. However, good teachers never fail to be cognizant of the diversity in their midst and are constantly reflective of their own teaching practices. Students in our classes will represent a wide array of human experience and some of those students will learn differently, communicate differently or access information in various ways. We can either expect them to adjust to us or we can think creatively and create a classroom that is inclusive of all. It is not up to students to fit into our narrow definitions of smart; it is up to all of us as TAs, teachers and professors to reach all of our students in ways that challenge and support them to show us all that they do know.

Zach Rossetti is a doctoral student in Special Education and Disability Studies at Syracuse University.

Christy Ashby is a doctoral student in Special Education and Disability Studies at Syracuse University.

References

Danforth, S. & Rhodes, W. (1997). Deconstructing disability: A philosophy for inclusion. *Remedial and Special Education,* 18, 357-366.

Donnellan, A. & Leary, M. (1995). *Movement differences and diversity in autism/mental retardation: Appreciating and accom modating people with communication and behavior challenges.* Madison, WI: DRI Press.

Gardner, H. (1983). *Frames of mind: The theory of multiple intelligences.* New York: Basic Books.

Goffman, E. (1963). *Stigma: Notes on the management of spoiled identity.* New York: Simon & Schuster, Inc.

Hardman, M., Drew, C., Egan, M. & Wolf, B. (1993). *Human Exceptionality: Society, school and family.* Needham Heights: Allyn and Bacon.

Hayman, R. (1998). *The smart culture: Society, intelligence, and law.* New York: New York University Press.

Heyward, W. (2000). *Exceptional Children: An introduction to special education.* Upper Saddle River: Prentice-Hall.

Heyward, W. (2003). *Exceptional Children: An introduction to special education.* Upper Saddle River: Prentice-Hall.

Kliewer, C. (1998). *Schooling children with Down syndrome: Toward an understanding of possibility.* New York: Teachers College Press

Ladson-Billings, G. (1994). *The dreamkeepers: Successful teachers of African American children.* San Francisco: Jossey-Bass Publishers.

Linton, S. (1998). *Claiming disability: Knowledge and identity.* New York: New York University Press.

Shapiro, J. P. (1993), *No Pity: People with disabilities forging a new Civil Rights movement.* New York: Three Rivers Press.

Tomlinson, C. (1999). *The differentiated classroom: Responding to the needs of all learners.* Alexandria, VA: Association for Supervision and Curriculum Development.

Tools for Universal Instruction

Thomas Argondizza

Teaching assistants face many exciting challenges; one of them is challenging students, especially as the student body continues to grow in size and in diversity. One factor in this growth is the many students with disabilities, both visible and invisible, including those with learning disabilities, physical and sensory disabilities. Making instructional materials accessible helps ensure that all students are equally challenged and have the same opportunity to succeed. One of the most direct ways we can make this happen is to use the principals of *universal instructional design* (UID) to help even the playing field among students. The application of UID not only assists those with disabilities, but also helps all learners understand instruction more clearly.

Instructional Design

Instructional design refers to the systematic and reflective process of translating principles of learning and instruction into plans for instructional materials, activities, information resources and evaluation (Ragan & Smith, 1999). Although the acting professor may determine course curriculum, teaching assistants can yield powerful influence when properly informed. One of the most important pieces of instructional design is a clear understanding of the audience through what is called a *learner analysis*. Just as a coat needs to fit the body of the wearer, instruction needs to fit the learner. An understanding of the learner helps form the instruction to come. Teaching assistants can be involved in lesson planning, test administration and facilitating discussion groups.

Universal Design

Universal design in instruction is an adaptation of the broader principals of universal design developed by the Center for Universal Design at North Carolina State University (Orkwis, 2003). Universal design principles describe how objects, such as doorways or machines, can be designed to allow access to all users. Following is a list of the principals and their meanings (Orkwis, 2003):

Equitable use: the design is useful and marketable to people with diverse abilities.

Flexibility in use: the design accommodates a wide range of individual preferences and abilities.

Simple and intuitive: use of the design is easy to understand, regardless of the user's experience, knowledge, language skills or current concentration level.

Perceptible information: the design communicates necessary information effectively to the user, regardless of existing conditions or the user's sensory abilities.

Tolerance for error: the design minimizes hazards and the adverse consequences of accidental or unintended actions.

Low physical effort: the design can be used efficiently and comfortably and with a minimum of fatigue.

Size and space for approach and use: appropriate size and space is provided for approach, reach, manipulation and use regardless of users' body size, posture or mobility.

In examining these seven principles, we can see that they share one common theme; they all allow users to operate properly regardless of their physical or cognitive abilities. The same theory is then applied to instruction, but it focuses on challenge rather than on operation or use.

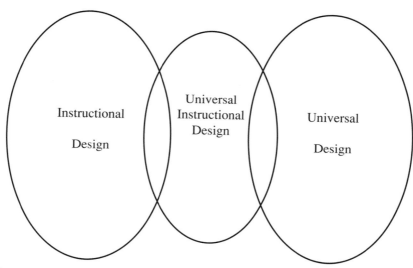

Figure 1.1 The relationship between instructional design, universal design, and universal instructional design.

Universal instructional design means the design of instructional materials and activities that make the learning goals achievable by individuals with wide differences in their abilities to see, hear, speak, move, read, write, understand English, attend, organize, engage and remember (Burgstahler, 2001). This universal design for learning is achieved through flexible materials and learning activities that include students with differing abilities. Below are suggestions for instructional methods that utilize the principles of universal design:

Equitable use: allow multiple options for students to demonstrate they have mastered the objectives required. Simply allowing several options for presentations—computer, handouts, use of overhead projector or role-playing—works well. This way, students with diverse abilities have equal opportunities to show they have mastered the required content. In the beginning of the semester, instructors can offer questionnaires, asking students for information about themselves. Instructors should be sure to ask about any disability-related accommodations that may be necessary, as well as preferred learning styles (visual, auditory etc.).

Flexibility in use: include more than one form of presentation material. For example, instructors can easily include both PowerPoint presentations and handouts in their lectures. This can help students who learn better through visual materials, and can help all students stay on track with the lesson. When facilitating lectures or discussion groups, instructors should read materials aloud. This benefits not only sight-impaired students, but also those who learn better through oral instruction.

Simple and intuitive use: clearly label all materials being used. When facilitating computer labs, instructors should ensure that control buttons are clear and within reach of all students.

Perceptible information: videos used during class should be captioned to include students with sensory disabilities and students for whom English may be a second language. If necessary instructors should have copies of course materials in Braille and in audio formats (these could be obtained by contacting the university's Office of Disability Services).

Tolerance for error: feedback helps us find correct performance as well as errors, which also offer the opportunity for learning. Instructors should provide effective feedback during class activities. If students use interpreters, instructors should make sure that interpreters are always present, allowing deaf students to demonstrate their abilities. This keeps the students on track and allows them to grasp concepts and to learn from mistakes or errors.

Low physical effort: keeping the office floor clear of clutter makes it more accessible to individuals who use mobility aids, such as wheelchairs or crutches.

Size and space for approach and use: When using a computer lab, instructors should check that keyboards are kept in a manner that will not impede wheelchairs from entering the desk spaces.

Distance Learning

Happily, we are seeing more and more use of distance learning applications not only in learning itself, but also in classroom-based teaching. Many courses now have online syllabi or discussion groups that allow students to interact and keep up with course-related events while off campus. These tools, however, may create barriers for those who are sight-impaired or who have certain forms of learning disabilities. Since the Americans with Disabilities Act (ADA) of 1990 requires that people with disabilities have equal access to public programs and services, instructors must make distance learning accessible to all students, regardless of disabilities.

There are some simple remedies these problems. Students who may be adversely affected by instruction through Web sites (for example, people with visual impairments), can use computers equipped with screen-reader software and speech synthesizers. Braille displays, which print text screens, may also be used. These tools are useful only for text screens; images and graphics cannot be detected. Web sites that are created for courses should be developed using text-based programs, not programs that use only images as the basis for sites. Instructors should advise students at the beginning of the semester that Web sites will be used and that diverse needs can be addressed.

Conclusion

Universal design can influence the design of instruction to

make it accessible to as many students as possible. By instruction, we mean a goal-directed teaching process, which is more or less pre-planned (Romiszowski, 1981). The two most important items in this type of pedagogy are flexibility and an open-door policy; these can make or break the accessibility of instruction. All instructors should plan flexibility into the design of classroom environments so changes can be made easily. Listening to students allows them to bring any needs they may have to the instructor's attention.

Thomas Argondizza is a Syracuse University graduate who works as an Instructional Designer in Maryland.

References

Burgstahler, S. (2001). Universal design of instruction. *Washington University DO-IT Web site.* Retrieved January 15, 2004, from the World Wide Web:http://www.washington.edu/doit

Orkwis, R. (2003). Universally designed instruction. *ERIC Clearing House on Disabilities and Gifted Education.* Retrieved January 15, 2004, from the World Wide Web: http://ericed.org

Ragan, T., & Smith, P. (1999). *Instructional Design.* New York: Wiley & Sons, Inc.

Romiszowski, A.J. (1981). *Designing Instructional Systems.* London: Kogan Page Ltd.

"Lame Idea": Disabling Language in the Classroom

Liat Ben-Moshe

As instructors, our job is to teach new material and prescribe new knowledge to our students. The way we choose to do this job is as significant as the educational content we are transmitting. As an instructor, a student and a person with a disability, I feel that it is up to all of us to convey our messages in ways that create the most comfortable and inclusive environment. Our classrooms should be safe places, not places that perpetuate oppression, exclusion and discrimination. The language that we use in the classroom is imperative for achieving these goals.

In the English language, using disability as a metaphor, an analogy and a derogatory term is common. Examples of such phrases and terms include: lame idea, blind justice, dumb luck, felt paralyzed, argument fell on deaf ears, crippling, crazy, insane, idiotic and retarded.

One might argue that using these words without relating them to particular individuals is not offensive. However, using disability as an analogy not only offends certain individuals, but it also impedes clear communication, perpetuates false beliefs about disability and creates an environment of unease and exclusion.

Disability Denotes Deficiency

Disability has negative connotation   en used

metaphorically, while the real experience of living with a disability can be quite enriching and empowering. In all the examples above disability is used in a value-laden way. "Lame idea" means bad idea or one that is not constructed in a sufficient and persuasive manner. When we call a notion or act "idiotic/moronic/ retarded" we are trying to convey the message that the idea or notion is ill-conceived, lacking in thought or unintelligent. When we describe someone as "blind" to a fact (for example, men are blind to sexist practices), we mean that they are lacking knowledge or have no notion of what transpires around them. "Crazy" means excessive or without control. None of these signifying phrases carries positive and empowering interpretations.

As educators, we must bear in mind that disability labels have a history, and that those labels have been highly contested over the decades. These words were actually created to describe people with different abilities as inferior within particular value systems. For instance, the words "moron," "idiot" and "imbecile" were used throughout the 20th century as medical classifications to denote different levels of intellectual deficiency. Later on, all these terms were conflated under the umbrella of "mental retardation" (Clark & Marsh, 2002).

The category of mental retardation, by itself, is highly contested for its reification of all perceived differences in cognitive abilities into one unified category. The important fact here is that mental retardation is a social construction, not a real condition that is innate in people's minds. The only requirement for inclusion in this category is deviation from a norm (usually prescribed by the use of IQ test) and perceived incompetence. Mental retardation is by itself a linguistic metaphor that means "cognitively delayed." When used metaphorically in everyday speech, "retarded" stands for slow or underdeveloped thought processes.

When we use terms like "retarded," "lame" or "blind"— even if we are referring to acts or ideas and not to people at all— we perpetuate the stigma associated with disability. By using a label which is commonly associated with disabled people to denote a deficiency, a lack or an ill-conceived notion, we reproduce the oppression of people with disabilities. As educators, we must be aware of the oppressive power of "everyday" language and try to change it.

False Beliefs Contained in Disabling Phrases

We learn about disability through everyday use of language. In the same way that racist or sexist attitudes, whether implicit or explicit, are acquired through the "normal" learning process, so too are negative assumptions about disabilities and the people who are labeled as having them. Our notions of people who are blind, deaf or labeled as mentally retarded come into play when we use disabling phrases, and these notions are usually far from accurate. They do not convey the complexity of living in a society that regards people with disabilities as the Other on the basis of perceived mentally or bodily difference.

The use of disability as a metaphor perpetuates false beliefs about the nature of impairment and disability. People who are blind, for example, do not lack in knowledge; they simply have different ways of obtaining it. Paralysis does not necessarily imply lack of mobility, stagnancy or dependence since there are augmentative instruments, such as wheelchairs and personal aids, that secure independence and mobility. The continued use of disabling language in the classroom perpetuates ignorance and misconceptions in regards to the lived experience of people with disabilities.

Power Relations in the Classroom

As Marxists, feminists and anti-racist activists and scholars have claimed for decades, the world is viewed mostly from the perspective of the rulers, and language is created in their image as well. Therefore, we must not be surprised that the use of disabling language not only persists, but is neither contested nor acknowledged. Disabling language is language that accepts the assumption that disabilities *are* bad, unfortunate or denote lack/deficiency; that they *are* invisible and insignificant to society as a whole; and that disabilities belong to the Other and are distinct from what we would term as normal.

What this language hides is that there is a power struggle of definitions, that normalcy is culturally determined and ever-changing, and that there are more people who are defined as having disabilities than we acknowledge. The question that disability activists and scholars are asking is not who is disabled, but who gets to be defined as blind, mentally retarded or crippled and under what power relations? Using an oppressive abelist language to denote deficiency reproduces the same hierarchy and power relations in the classroom, and renders these phrases unproblematic.

Disability is not a metaphor. It is an identity.

Using disability as a metaphor to represent only negative aspects of a situation is problematic. It is made worse by the fact that blindness, deafness, paralysis, etc., are not floating signifiers, but have real referents behind them—people with disabilities. When using disabling language, we do not only de-value the lived experience of people with disabilities, but we also appropriate these lived experiences for our own use. This means that disabled people have been presented as socially flawed able-bodied people, not as people with our own identities. As responsible instructors, we must ask ourselves, when was the last time we discussed disability in our classrooms, not as metaphors, but as lived experiences?

The consequences of this exclusion are that most students know disability only metaphorically (unless they have disabilities themselves), and that we fail them as teachers by not providing descriptions of what disability actually means to the people who embody it. As critical teachers, we should counteract the use of disability as a metaphor in everyday language, in media and in literary representations. This pedagogical goal can be achieved by introducing more complex accounts of the disability experience through autobiographies, guest speakers or critical accounts by people with disabilities or by scholars of disability studies.

To make matters more complex, we must consider that some of our students might have disabilities themselves. These can be hidden and not visible. When we use disabling language, we alienate our students from our arguments and from feeling included in the classroom. As a wheelchair user, I find that when people use terms like "crippling" or "disabling" as rhetorical devices, I am distracted from the discussions. I cannot listen to arguments that make their point by using my identity as a rhetorical device. When a student tells me, "'I didn't know what do. I was paralyzed," I think to myself, "funny, I'm paralyzed, but I do know what to do." I stop listening to my student's complaint and feel offended by the conversation. When this happens, I feel "mugged by a metaphor" in the words of Wahneema Lubiano (1996). [1]

Talking About People with Disabilities Not as Metaphors

Disability is socially constructed and engulfs many labels under its umbrella. Although people with different impairments and disability labels are not similar in their thoughts, feelings or everyday lives, they are united under an oppressive label. The effects of being labeled as disabled have profound implications on disabled individuals in the areas of employment, education, built environment and product design, leisure activities, politics, family and sexual lives. "Disability," therefore, represents a complex system of social constraints imposed on people with impairments by a highly discriminatory society; to be disabled

---

[1] Lubiano is talking about the metaphor of muticulturalsm and the inequality produced by racial relations, and the way she experiences these effects on her indiviuality as a black woman. Although we do not share the same social location, I can empathize with her.

means being discriminated against. The problem is even more
comlex for disabled members of other marginalized locales such
as the gay and lesbian communities, people of color and women.

How can we refer to disability as an identity and to the
people who embody this identity and not be offensive? What
follows is a list of terms currently in use by activists, academics
and the media to refer to people with bodily or mental difference.

Disabled people

This is most commonly used in Great Britain.
Traditionally, it was thought that innate medical conditions
defined disability status and caused exclusion. As Laurence Clark
and Stephen Marsh recall, "In the mid-seventies a new way of
thinking about disability emerged from the disabled people's civil
rights movement called the social model of disability. This stated
that disabled people are those people with impairments who
experience barriers within society. Therefore, the term 'disabled
people' was redefined by the movement to mean "people with
impairments who are disabled by socially constructed barriers"
(2002, p. 2). "Disablement," therefore, refers to prejudice,
stereotyping or "institutional discrimination" against disabled
people.

People with disabilities

This is the most commonly used descriptor in the United
States. It is used by disability rights activists and scholars. Like
the term "disabled people," the phrase "people with disabilities"
emerged from the disability movement in the United States where
people-first phrasing was coined. The tendency to place the noun
"people" before "disability" is viewed positively because it
emphasizes the fact that individuals with impairments are, first
and foremost, people—something which historically has been
denied.

deaf/Deaf

Most deaf people do not identify themselves as disabled,

but consider deaf people a linguistic minority; they simply use sign instead of oral communications. Some Deaf people have also adopted a capital "D" in order to show their affiliation with Deaf culture and to politicize the word.

Handicapped or mentally handicapped

These terms alludes to a time when people with disabilities were viewed mostly as beggars who went "cap in hand" (Barnes, 1992). The use of "mentally handicapped," "feebleminded" or "retarded" has been replaced in the United States with the phrases "people with intellectual disabilities" or "people with developmental disabilities." These phrases are preferred terms by people who have been labeled in those ways, as well as by activists and scholars.

Challenged

Phrases based on "politically correct" language started to replace terms like "the handicapped" in the 1980s. Referring to impairment as "challenging" portrays them as obstacles to be overcome. However, these phrases ignore the disabling social barriers, placing the emphasis instead on impairments as the "challenging" factor (Clark & Marsh, 2002). In the US, this phrase is often used as a euphemism, such as the phrase 'vertically challenged' to refer to people who are short. The type of usage is generally considered patronizing. The phrase "physically challenged" also brings to mind the super-crip narrative of people with disabilities who climb mountains or are literary geniuses in spite of their "severe disabilities." Being physically challenged for able-bodied people and disabled people should be a matter of choice. We hope that *all* our students are intellectually challenged by the courses they take.

Special needs

"The phrase 'special needs' came about as an attempt to demedicalize the labeling of disabled children, changing it to what was hoped to be less negative labeling based on educational need"

(Reiser & Mason, 1990, in Clark & Marsh, 2002, p. 12). "The 'needs' referred to here are typically determined by professional assessment, rather than by disabled people themselves" (Clark & Marsh, 2002, p. 12). Often these needs are commonplace: for example, disabled children "need" to receive a decent education, just like any other children. However, "the disabling culture transforms ordinary human needs into special needs and corrupts the identity of disabled children into special needs children" (Finklestein & Stuart, 1996).

Value-laden terms

"Emotive terms relating to disabled people, such as 'afflicted,' 'restricted,' 'stricken,' 'sufferer,' 'unfortunate' and 'victim,' tend to reflect a person's negative reactions to a disabled person" (Clark & Marsh, 2002, p. 6). Describing a person as being "afflicted" by blindness or a "victim" of cerebral palsy takes away the agency from the individual and gives an active role to a constructed condition (Linton, 1998). Similarly, terms like "wheelchair bound" and "confined to a wheelchair" are value-laden and inaccurate, since wheelchairs are devices that empower rather than restrict the people who use them. Since paralysis or blindness do not have signifiers of their own, the augmentative devices attached to them (like canes or wheelchairs) carry the disabling stigma. In addition, many wheelchair users can walk short distances, and, therefore, are not "bound" to wheelchairs.

Conclusion

The language that we use in our classrooms has far-reaching implications on the education of students. Just as we would not tolerate sexist, misogynist or racist language, we must not tolerate disabling imagery and phrases. In particular, we should not contribute to reproducing it. Disability is not merely a metaphor or an analogy, but it is an identity for some of us as well as for some of our students. Disability is defined almost arbitrarily and the line between the disabled and the nondisabled is not a clear one. We must not assume disability, or the lack of it, by mere observation. Abelist language can be offensive and hurt some of our students while interfering with our original messages. We can either create barriers to communication or we can create classrooms in which we *all* feel equally challenged.

Liat Ben-Moshe is a Ph.D. student in Sociology, Disability Studies and Women Studies at Syracuse University.

References

Barnes, C. (1992). *Disabling imagery and the media: An exploration of the principles for media representations of disabled people*. Derby: The British Council of Disabled People.

Clark, L. and Marsh, S. (2002). *Patriarchy in the UK: The language of disability*. Retrieved from the World Wide Web: http://www.leeds.ac.uk/disability-studies/archiveuk/titles.html

Finklestein, V. and Stuart, O. (1996). Developing new services. In Hales,G. (Ed.), *Beyond Disability: Towards an enabling society*. London: Sage Publications.

Linton, S. (1998). *Claiming Disability*. New York: New York University Press.

Lubiano, W. (1996). Like being mugged by a metaphor: Multiculturalism and state narratives. In Gordon and Newfield (Eds.), *Mapping Multiculturalism*. Minneapolis: University of Minnesota Press.

Reiser, R. (2001). Does language matter? *Disability Tribune*, October 2001.

Learning from Each Other: Syracuse University and the OnCampus Program

Cheryl G. Najarian
Michele Paetow

For many students with disabilities, the ordinary ritual of graduating from high school with classroom friends never happens. Instead, these students typically stay at their high schools until they turn twenty-one and then transition to the world of adult service agencies, where there are few opportunities to further their academic interests. Fortunately, for a small number of students in the Syracuse City School District, there is now an alternative.

In the spring of 2000, local parents and disability activists, Ro and Joe Vargo, learned of a college-based program in Kentucky that allows students with significant needs for support in special education to attend college classes. Their daughter was about to graduate from a local high school and she needed this type of opportunity. With the support of Doug Biklen, professor of Cultural Foundations of Education, and leaders from the Syracuse City School District, OnCampus (OC) was created for six students aged eighteen to twenty-one.

Now in its fourth year, the OnCampus program is considered the next logical, inclusive step for a school district nationally recognized for its ability to educate children of all ability levels in heterogeneous classrooms. Nondisabled students who participated in the program say they better understand issues of diversity. They have also started questioning medical definitions of disability, ideas about intelligence and the ways in which we obtain knowledge.

Preliminary studies show that all students, regardless of whether they have disabilities, can benefit from such an enhanced overall learning environment. Given this, we would like to share our experiences with OnCampus in hopes that our story will encourage other instructors to incorporate the principals and theories of the program into their own undergraduate classrooms.

Reflections

The six OnCampus students each have a customized schedule, formed by their personal goals and interests. Under the supervision of a teacher and teaching assistants, students audit two classes each semester, participate in social and recreational activities with SU undergraduates and participate in vocational training at sites around the SU campus. To get a better understanding of the program, let us begin with a few reflections from instructors and students who participated in this initial class.

Cheryl, an instructor's, remembrances:

I was first made aware of the OC program when I became an instructor of my own course, Sociology of Families, in the fall semester of 2002, and I have worked with the program ever since. As a sociologist and educator who both studies and teaches issues of disability, race, gender and social class, I saw the inclusion of these students into my classroom as a unique opportunity to create a classroom space that visibly reflected some of the things that I ask my students to question, such as definitions of ability. To be entirely honest, I did not give much thought to how I would work to include these students or how this would happen in my classroom.

Instead, my approach was to think about how to build a classroom community with *all* of the individuals in the class—SU and OC students alike—so that everyone could benefit from the experience. By working closely with students, the OC teaching assistants, and the director of the program, I believe we were able to create such a community.

Building a classroom that is a safe space is important in any learning environment, and perhaps even more critical when discussing things such as the family, which connects so closely with our personal lives. One thing that I did and I continue to do is to reserve the first week of classes for introductions, expectations, the syllabus and my classroom contract. Students may not know it, but my aim in that first week is to create the foundation for a community, which evolves over the course of the semester. In this way, they know that I take what they will learn from this community as seriously as the information they will learn from the texts in our course. I view each student in my class as an equal contributor and I model this by asking them to all be part of a group presentation in which they teach the class. By creating this atmosphere in the classroom, I believe we are able to, as a class, learn more about the sociological concepts of the family, gender, work and theories of disability and ability.

Perhaps one of the biggest challenges in any classroom is getting students to do their best. I challenge them to do this during the first week and let them know that only they know if they are really trying their hardest. I encourage them to take ownership of this. Working with OC has enhanced my classroom communities by teaching diversity and sociology in ways that textbooks often cannot. By simply making all students feel that they have a stake in our learning environment, I have found, to my delight, that what develops is understanding and respect for people of all abilities. This may sound idealistic to some, however, I have found that if expectations are set high, students are eager to reach and, often, exceed expectations. Having a classroom contract and going over expectations are ways of setting some ground rules. However, I also ask students to discuss their own expectations and set the boundaries for our discussions.

Michele, an OnCampus teacher's, thoughts:

Meeting the tremendous variety of needs in a typical classroom is not something most teachers can do. In many inclusive classrooms, special education teachers change the assignments or design separate activities for students with disabilities that parallel classroom instruction. This add-on approach to curriculum is improved when a teacher uses the concept of universal design and makes lesson plans based on the assumption that all students will need multiple ways to find meaning in the material.

In our sociology classroom at Syracuse University, our instructor defined a clear ethos of high expectation and acceptance. All students were valued and respected equally as intellectually curious and capable. Upon this foundation of safety, OnCampus students grew comfortable, more confident and willing to attempt the challenging assignments of the course. In one class, James, a freshman and an OnCampus student, commented, "This isn't a special education program, is it? Because I don't do that."

What is significant about this comment is that the environment successfully deconstructed the deficit-driven model of traditional "special education" for this student. Special education for James had become a label and an environment to avoid because it represented a demeaning concept, placing him at the lowest rungs of the social order. Remarkably, he did not feel that in this college classroom.

As the supervising teacher from the Syracuse City School District, I work with SU instructors to make curriculum accessible and meaningful for OnCampus students. This process begins with a discussion with the instructor about each student's learning style and some of the major themes and ideas to be taught in the class. Sociology of Families is rich with material that is applicable and relevant to all students. I found the ideas, the text and the format of the class widely accessible to learners with developmental disabilities. Cheryl's teaching philosophy of inclusion set a tone of acceptance and understanding regarding any changes that I needed to make for our students. Based on the needs of the learner, and in collaboration with the class instructor, I adapted the curricular goals for this course using one or more of the following strategies:

Size: I reduced the number of items or the length of the paper that the student is expected to complete.

Difficulty: I adapted the instruction by simplifying the language or the concept. I simplified task directions and changed the rules to accommodate learner needs.

Time: I extended the time allotted for students to complete assignments.

Substitute curriculum: I provided supplemental instruction and different materials to meet individualized goals. For example, rather than writing an essay on parenting styles, one OnCampus student constructed a survey and wrote a paragraph that summarized th data and presented this to the class.

Voices from the classroom

In the fall of 2003, we created a survey and distributed it to both the SU and OC students in the Sociology of Families class. We asked students to comment on how, if at all, being part of a classroom community which included undergraduate students at SU and students from OC shaped their learning experiences and ideas about disability. What follows are some statements by students in the class:

> After hearing one of the OnCampus program's students speak through a machine to the class, I realized just how much he was learning from his classmates. It opened my eyes to people with disabilities. I think all classrooms should be open to people with disabilities because, like the case in our class, these students are learning from us as well as we are learning from them.
>
> *Renee, senior, psychology major*

> It adds a great deal to the class.   School is all about learning.   I've learned a great deal from this experience.
> *Karen, sophomore, public relations and sociology major*

> To other teachers who may be concerned, I would say that OnCampus students are just like other students.
> *Jason, freshman, OC*

> Learning about all types of diversity is important to the college experience.   SU has recognized that. However, the disabled are often left out of the term "diversity," so, therefore, incorporation of this program is beneficial.
> *Lisa, junior, biology and women's studies major*

We can see from these comments how building such a classroom community aided our students in learning from each other and helped them develop ideas about definitions of "diversity." Students were able to think about the sociological concepts of "difference" and how "norms" and exceptions for these ideologies are created by social institutions, such as the family. As the students began to question how we have come to know what we know about the family, they also began challenging societal notions of disability, ability, work, gender and the development of inequalities. By understanding inequality and stratification in our society, students are in a better position to think more carefully about how to possibly create social change with regards to some of the ideologies, laws and policies that keep these inequities in place.

They also developed some ideas about respect:

> Respect the time it takes to respond to questions, to get the answer I want. I can't always get a teacher to teach people to respect me.
>
> *Mike, sophomore, OC*

> I think teachers should definitely include this program because it shows them that this is how the world is. Accept it! Learn from it. These students can probably teach us more than any textbook.
>
> *Jessica, freshman, broadcast journalism major*

> It helps me to see that disability doesn't mean you can't do something. It just means you have to be willing to look outside the box and figure out different ways to do something. This includes learning. Being disabled doesn't mean you can't go to college; it just means you have to be open to alternative styles of learning.
>
> *Laura, junior, broadcast journalism major*

> Not too nice, calling us disabled when we have so many abilities. Respect doesn't come from a name; it comes from not ignoring needs.
>
> *Danny, freshman, OC*

These comments highlight two major themes, which we would argue are beneficial outcomes of having such a classroom environment. As the students mention, this classroom created a space where they learned from each other and taught each other about respect. As the students learned about each other, they were able to question major sociological concepts from the class such as ability, race, class and gender and how these concepts shape our definitions of a family. Thus, having such a classroom dynamic had two major benefits: it enhanced the ability of the students to absorb the class materials; and students, as they learned about their colleagues, were able to question our general society's definitions of what it means to be able or disabled.

Strategies for a classroom community

Informed by our own experiences and the work of Tomlinson (2003) on differentiating instruction, we offer the following suggestions for teaching academically diverse learners:

Curriculum should be coherent, inviting and well thought out assuming a strength-based model of different learning styles.

Tasks and assignments should respect the individual learner. Students should all be expected to think at high levels. Instructors should teach in ways that activate students' background knowledge on topics and then assist students in putting together their classroom lessons to form new structures or concepts.

Instructors should use a variety of student groupings, allowing students to demonstrate academic and social competencies alone, in pairs and with a variety of their classroom peers.

Students should be graded in ways that acknowledge growth, effort and their personal bests.

Instructors should assume a posture of collaboration with any resource or support staff available.

Conclusion

We have shared our story of how working together, as an instructor at SU and the director of the OC program, we have built a successful classroom community. Certainly, these efforts were not without some challenges; however, we found that the first step in achieving an inclusive classroom was to work together to have OC and SU students share classroom spaces. Merging the two groups into one classroom enabled SU students and students in the OC program to learn from each other and better understand the course material. We would like our success to serve as a challenge and an example for instructors who are interested in incorporating this experience into their own classrooms. We conclude with some questions that we hope will help push instructors beyond this first step of inclusion:

What might an inclusive model of education look like at the institutional level in terms of policy changes?

How can we get our students more involved in making and creating this policy?

In what other ways can teachers use this experience to enhance learning for both students and educators alike?

For more information on becoming involved with OnCampus students or for more information on the inclusion of students with disabilities in classes at SU, please contact:

OnCampus Coordinator
School of Education
373 Huntington Hall
Syracuse, NY 13244-2340
315-443-9683

*At the time of writing this chapter, Cheryl G. Najarian taught in
the Department of Sociology and Women's Studies Program at
Syracuse University and is now an Assistant Professor of
Sociology at the University of Massachusetts Lowell.*

*Michele Paetow directs the Syracuse City School District
OnCampus program of Syracuse University.*

References

Armstrong, T. (1994). *Multiple intelligences in the classroom.*
Alexandria: Association of Supervision and Curriculum
Development.

Biklen, D. (1992). *Schooling without labels.* Philadelphia: Temple
University Press.

Gardner, H. (1983). *Frames of mind: The theory of multiple
intelligences.* United States: Basic Books.

Meyer, A. & Rose, D.H. (1998). *Learning to read in the computer
age.* Cambridge: Brookline Books.

Meyer, A. & Rose, D.H. (2002). *Teaching every student in the
digital age: Universal design for learning.* Alexandria:
Association for Supervision and Curriculum Development.

Tomlinson, C. A. (2003). Differentiating in practice: A
resource guide for differentiating curriculum. *Educational
Leadership.* October, pp. 7-11.

III.
Students with Disabilities in the Classroom

Being an Ally

Katrina Arndt
Pat English-Sand

What is an ally? Does being an ally mean we have to befriend all people in the group with which we want to associate ourselves? Does it mean we have to agree with everything a person or group represents? Is being an ally about helping? Can we be allies with groups in which we do not belong? Is the role of ally supporting a political agenda? These are a few of the questions that come to mind when we think about our roles as allies to people with disabilities and the disability rights movement as a whole. We ask ourselves these questions because there are no clear answers. Through dialogue with those with whom we ally ourselves, we can answer some of these questions and develop our identities in this evolving and complex role.

Although there are a number of definitions for ally, we must choose one that we feel comfortable with and that fits within the context of the group with which we ally ourselves, in this case disability. The context is important due to the complex political and philosophical perspective unique to this, or to any group. We have chosen to focus on what we consider the essential element of the definition, that there exist shared principles and beliefs around which both the ally and individual seeking an ally are willing to take action. This definition answers a few of our initial questions. We do not have to share friendship or agree upon every position, nor must we be insiders to be allies. We need only the shared principle or belief. At various times in our lives, we have both asked ourselves, "Why have we aligned ourselves with disability rights groups?" Neither of us identifies as having a disability, nor are we able to identify a personal incident or experience that has connected us to disability groups. We are outsiders. What we recognize, however, is an awareness of beliefs and principles surrounding disability that are similar to how we feel about any oppressed group; our concern is borne of a strong commitment to civil rights.

   The continuing struggle we have in our roles as allies with individuals with disabilities is how to be members of the group when we do not share the element that brings the members together. Historically, in the United States, individuals with disabilities have been treated as if they cannot speak for themselves. This makes us hyper-aware of how we speak and represent ourselves to this group and to others.

   While we do not share the same experiences as our colleagues with disabilities, we are citizens in the same society and participants in the democratic process that affects all of us. Our participation in disability rights groups is similar to white Americans participating in the civil rights movement. Our role is to participate with our peers with disabilities in the democratic process. Our participation may include educating others, challenging policy, protesting exclusionary practice or celebrating gains toward equity. The following two examples of our experiences as allies to colleagues with disabilities illustrate the complex nature of the role.

Miriam

   Miriam uses a wheelchair. She gets around campus a lot differently than we do. We walk around campus freely, up and down the hills. She drives from building to building and parks in the "handicapped" space if it is available; sometimes it is not, but mostly it is.

   In the winter, when there is a great deal of snow, Miriam

has more difficulty. The building and grounds staff plow and shovel regularly, yet there are times when Miriam misses class because she can not physically get to the building. She prepares. She does the reading, gets her notes together and spends a lot of time and energy preparing for our seminars. Still, she misses class even though she leaves home, drives to campus, gets out of the car and gets into her wheelchair. She is physically unable to get onto the sidewalk due to snow. Miriam is not lazy or blowing off class. She tries to get there; she cannot. So she drives home and e-mails the professors, who are understanding and frustrated—not with her, but with the situation. Then she tamps down the frustration she feels at being unable to get where she needs to go. Because it's happened before, and will probably happen again.

Here is where the ally part comes in. We have a different type of frustration. We are in Miriam's classes, and we know when she has a missed class; we have missed her. When we learn why she has missed classes, we become angry. We know that Miriam has notified buildings and grounds about her schedule. We know her and know that she has called over and over and asked for what should be a standard matter of course: clear access to class.

We act as Miriam's allies in several ways: we start generating conversation within the Beyond Compliance Coordinating Committee (BCCC) about snow removal, and why it is important; we offer to call buildings and grounds ourselves, as a number of complaints may result in quicker response, we commiserate with her, get her copies of the notes for the missed lecture and discussion, and assure her she is not alone in this struggle for access. We are with Miriam. We don't speak or take action for her, but we are with her. Being an ally means dealing with the issue so that she is not dealing with it by herself. We want Miriam to feel that we are invested in the issue of snow removal, that we support her efforts to get to class, and that while we can't completely understand her experience, we can do our best to support her efforts toward change.

Kelly

A second example of being an ally involves Kelly, a colleague who uses interpreters. Again, we took many classes together and were familiar with the protocol of interpreters arriving a few minutes before class. Seven or eight of us sat in a group; we had been assigned to work together for the semester and were getting to know each other well. One night, the interpreters did not show up before class. As class time arrived and the professor began to lecture, there was still no interpreter. We were not sure what to do, but wanted to be supportive of Kelly. We looked to Kelly; she wanted to wait a few minutes. The rest of us discussed what we should do. We talked about the possibility of leaving class as a group; if our colleague could not access class, than none of us was willing to stay. We shared that option with Kelly. We discussed saying something to the professor about the need to wait to lecture until the interpreter arrived. Kelly decided that before taking action she wanted to wait a few minutes to see if the interpreter came, so we did. We hope that we conveyed our support, as her allies, for her in this situation. As it turned out, the interpreter was late but did arrive.

The biggest part of being an ally is being present and sharing the struggle or success. While we can get to class and listen to lectures without interpreters, it is important to us to be sure that our colleagues with disabilities are also able to get to class and access the lectures. Being an ally means understanding the barriers and working to eliminate them. While we do that, we are constantly guided by our colleagues to act in accordance with their goals and plans, not by our own. The hardest part of being an ally is to constantly check what we are doing against what our colleagues have to say. We are not directing the action, but we are doing what we are directed to do. The power of making decisions must reside with the people the work is designed to support. All too often we have heard about groups being taken over by people who are not members of the group. As allies, we are not members of the group of people with disabilities. We are allies: non-members who are here to provide support not drive the agenda.

As instructors, we carry these same thoughts and opinions with us into our classrooms—in how we approach our teaching, organize our instruction and classroom, and interact with our students. We know that not all disabilities are visible and that many students will not disclose their disabilities to their instructors out of concern for being treated differently. We feel strongly that, based on our own convictions on this topic as well as the university required Americans With Disabilities Act (ADA) compliance, we must serve as allies to our students. As teachers think about their positions on this topic and contemplate the combined roles of instructor and ally, we encourage them to consider the following suggestions:

Before the semester begins

Plan lectures in advance, so that copies of handouts are available prior to lectures.

Think about whether any videos have closed captioning in them, and learn how to use the equipment in your classrooms.

Think about accessibility of your classroom for students who use wheelchairs, and be prepared to ask that your class be moved.

Include on your syllabus a statement outlining how students can access supports through the Office for Disability Services (ODS).

During the semester

Tell students that you provide a safe environment for all students, and do so. This includes how you speak, how you lecture, and how you respond to comments by students that may be inappropriate.

Ask students how you can support them; many are not willing to disclose their disabilities based on previous negative experiences. Honor students' needs when they bring you documents for accommodations from ODS.

Incorporate into your planning the need to prepare some

accommodations ahead of time. Arrange for closed captioning for any videos. Think about how to make overhead handouts accessible for students with visual impairments. Consult with ODS.

Know how to access technology that makes your curriculum accessible. This might include closed captioning, Braille, electronic formatted texts or handouts. Find out where on campus you can get the supports you need. Be able to find the department you need to ask for these types of supports for your students. Be able to get information on how to use them in your classroom.

Be aware of the physical layout of the classroom. Is it accessible?   Can every student participate in every lesson? Include disability in instruction and discussions; when you use an example, think about including examples that relate to disability.

Check the language/metaphors you use in your teaching. Do not use phrases like "that's lame." That reinforces the idea that there is something wrong with having a disability.

Admit when you do not know something. There is nothing wrong with asking for information or support.

Admit when you are uncomfortable. If you are uncomfortable about having a student with a disability in your class, acknowledge that and ask for help.

Being an ally means that we feel strongly enough about inequities for individuals with disabilities that we get involved in a way that conveys respect for individual autonomy, avoids pity and promotes our desire for equity. As instructors, our students deserve equal access in the classroom and it is our responsibility to ensure that this occurs. Syracuse University policies require that instructors make classrooms safe spaces for all students to learn. We hope you consider being an ally more than just implementing policy in the classroom.

Katrina Arndt is a doctoral student in Special Education at Syracuse University.

Pat English-Sand is a teacher of students with special needs, an inclusion facilitator, and a doctoral student in Special Education and Disability Studies at Syracuse University.

Adapting and "Passing": My Experiences as a Graduate Student with Multiple Invisible Disabilities

Elizabeth Sierra-Zarella

To most students and faculty members on the campus of Syracuse University, I am no different thaen anyone else. Some might think it odd that I wear sunglasses daily and long sleeves even in warm weather, but otherwise, I blend right in. My disabilities are invisible and because they are so well- hidden, people tend to be critical about my handicapped license plate and Quad parking privileges. Few know that I suffer from chronic pain and adult-onset asthma that severely limit my mobility. They cannot see my clinical depression and post-traumatic stress disorder. They are unaware that I am highly photosensitive and may be vulnerable to skin cancer due to advanced vitiligo, a hereditary autoimmune disorder that destroys the pigment cells. I am well on my way to becoming a complete albino.

Mine is not an unusual case. Many people with invisible disabilities succeed at "passing" as able-bodied, and we all have our own reasons for doing so. Denial, shame, social stigma and stubborn defiance against our own limitations motivate many invisibly disabled people to conceal the true nature of their disabilities, even to the point of avoiding assistance from the campus Office of Disability Services (ODS). Society, in general, recognizes disability only when assistive devices, such as wheelchairs or oxygen tanks, are required   ruth, unseen disabilities are just as real and debilitating as those that require the use of assistive technology.

Unfortunately, few able-bodied people understand the concept of "passing" while living with invisible disabilities. We must continually explain ourselves and the flexibility we require to our family, friends, coworkers, colleagues and, occasionally, even to total strangers. Instead of societal acknowledgement of the very existence of our disabling conditions, we are often looked upon with an air of suspicion and called on to explain, yet again, exactly why we think we need any accommodations. Our original disabling conditions are compounded with the resultant exasperation, stress and, sometimes, depression of living under constant scrutiny when all we wish to do is live our lives to the fullest extent possible. College campuses are especially difficult environments. As a newly appointed teaching assistant and a person with invisible disabilities, I hope to offer insight into how instructors can make classrooms and teaching methodologies as inclusive and accessible as possible.

Understanding

Like many people with invisible disabilities, I have learned to adapt to the environment at Syracuse University, where I am a graduate student. I show no outward expressions of the pain I have lived with for most of my life and I have learned to control my actions and movements to minimize the amount of pain I must experience on a daily basis. I conscientiously avoid most of my asthma-attack triggers and I use my maintenance and rescue inhalers quickly and efficiently. I control my psychiatric disabilities with medication, counseling, and regular medical checks with my doctor. As for the vitiligo, I hide my stark white hair with permanent dyes and always wear sunglasses and long sleeves when I am outdoors.

I can control my disabling conditions most of the time, but not always. There are times when changes in medication, physical well-being and environment making learning more difficult. However, no one can see the obstacles I face. Unless I feel comfortable enough to talk with an instructor about the necessity of accommodations, I will struggle to succeed. Instructors must be approachable. Thoughtful examination of disability issues leads to a greater understanding of and empathy for those who persevere despite physical, psychological and learning disabilities. Notice that I used the word "empathy," not "sympathy." Empathy involves being aware of and, as much as possible, vicariously experiencing the feelings of another without pity or condescension. This deeper sense of understanding and caring can serve instructors well in and out of the classroom as they form pedagogical practices.

Flexibility

New instructors will learn very quickly that many of us with chronic disabling conditions must live flexibly in anticipation of the changing nature of our disabilities. It is a matter of "bad days" and "better days" for many of us, myself included. As a result, we need our worlds to be flexible as well. Instructors should never assume that because students sometimes need none of their requested accommodations, they will not need them in the future. For example, due to my chronic pain condition, it is difficult for me to stay seated for long periods of time without experiencing a great deal of pain. As a result, I usually inform my instructors of my need for the freedom to take short breaks as needed. However, sometimes I can tolerate my pain long enough to make it through entire three- to four-hour classes. I find that taking occasional breaks might ease my physical pain, but that it interrupts the learning process and removes me from any classroom discussion that might be taking place. As a result, I take extra breaks only when absolutely necessary.

Since needs might change from day to day, it is important that the freedom to use any previously approved classroom adaptations continues to exist. It is also imperative that students have leeway to make necessary adaptations to requested accommodations as needed in the case of changing conditions.

Confidentiality

Often, students feel more comfortable coming to teaching assistants with personal concerns than to professors, especially in large lecture-style classes in which professors are distant figures. Teaching assistants might also be closer in age to most students than professors; that alone might make them more accessible confidantes. Both teaching assistants and professors should remember to be discreet at all times when students confide in them. They should listen with compassion when students describe their situations and realize that for some of us, admitting that we need special considerations at all is a major step. Teaching assistants should inform their professors when they learn that students need accommodations, but they should first make sure the students are comfortable with such a discussion. They should respect the privacy of students and allow them to approach their disabling conditions on their own terms. Instructors should be aware of and suggest, but not push, known community and campus resources.[1] Above all, they should conduct classes in a welcoming, non-judgmental manner to encourage those who need assistance to seek it out.

Accommodations

The type of accommodations necessary for students with invisible disabilities to succeed depends upon the nature and extent of the disabilities. There are generally three classes of invisible disabilities among student populations: physical, learning-related and psychological. The following is a brief synopsis of each and their most commonly requested accommodations:

Physical Disabilities

Invisible physical disabilities include chronic pain conditions, cardiovascular ailments, hearing and visual

---

[1] See **Informational Links** at the end of this article.

impairment, respiratory disorders, epilepsy, lupus and many other seriously debilitating conditions. A commonly requested accommodation among this population is the freedom to take extra breaks during class as needed without having this accommodation called to the rest of the students' attention. This avoids embarrassment and the implication of favoritism.

Some physical conditions, such as chronic pain and epilepsy, necessitate the use of medications that can seriously impair functioning until the optimal dosage is established. In cases like this, students might need extra excused absences while they go through the adjustment process for a necessary medication. This is a reasonable request. If a surgical or other therapeutic intervention is required during the semester, students might need to finish their coursework after the semester's end. In these cases, the granting of "incompletes" allows the students to finish courses without having to drop out due. Likewise, flexible exam scheduling may be needed due to conflicting medical appointments, complications with the medical condition or for other legitimate reasons.

Learning Disabilities

Learning disabilities are the most common invisible disability on campus. Students with learning disabilities have incredibly diverse needs that cannot be adequately addressed in this article. Some of the more recognized learning disorders are dyslexia, attention deficit hyperactivity disorder (ADHD) and attention deficit disorder (ADD). Students with these disorders may have difficulty dealing with the structure and function of classroom learning and might require extensive external assistance. While many people with learning disabilities control their disorders with medication and counseling, classroom accommodations are frequently necessary to facilitate their academic performance.

Due to the extensive nature of the accommodations needed by people with learning disabilities, these students will most likely work through ODS for assistance with note-taking, exam accommodations and tutoring. However, instructors can make their classrooms more accessible for people with learning disabilities by minimizing classroom distractions and working cooperatively with ODS to address any other needs.

Self-awareness of teaching methods and continual improvement can go a long way towards creating a welcoming learning environment for students with learning disabilities. For example, some students with learning disabilities have a difficult time following fast-paced complicated blackboard examples or PowerPoint presentations. The provision of printed versions of these teaching tools with the concepts concisely explained can assist students with learning disabilities to understand the subject matter with less difficulty.

By simply making themselves available to students for further explanation and patient discussion, instructors can greatly assist their students with learning disabilities. Such discussions allow instructors opportunities to solicit feedback and take reasonable suggestions for changes to pedagogical approaches seriously. Such suggestions are not personal affronts. Rather, they are an opportunity to reach all students more effectively.

Psychological Disabilities

Those of us with psychological disabilities are the least likely to self-identify. The persistent stigma against those with psychological disabilities prevents many students who need accommodations, assistance or treatment from seeking it out. Even those who do seek treatment can be highly reluctant to admit to this type of disability and will usually come to instructors for help in the classroom only when it becomes clear that there is no other option.

Instructors must realize that students risk a lot by revealing that they have psychologically disabling conditions. Some fear being thought of as dangerous, unstable or inferior. Many also hide their conditions to protect their reputations, families and careers from societal prejudice. The general misunderstanding of this form of disability among many people leads those of us who have psychological disabilities to keep it a secret to everyone but a select few.

Common psychological disorders include clinical depression, bipolar disorder, anxiety disorders (including post-traumatic stress disorder, obsessive-compulsive disorder and phobias), schizophrenia and borderline personality disorder. These conditions can be permanent or temporary, slight or severe. A basic knowledge of the most common psychological disabilities can be gained from freshman-level psychology texts, advocacy Web sites and the resources available at university counseling centers.

Most of us successfully manage our psychological disabilities through medication and counseling and require few classroom adaptations outside of an accepting and supportive environment. However, due to the nature of some psychological disorders, a student may find it difficult or impossible to attend class as regularly as his or her classmates. In addition, some psychotropic medications can be quite disorienting and may require a long period of adjustment when they are added or changed by the student's physician. A change in therapists or therapeutic methods can cause quite a bit of disruption in the student's life as well. Therefore, it may be necessary to allow extra excused absences, flexible exam scheduling and the granting of "incompletes" to allow these students to achieve at an optimal level.

Conclusion

Invisible disabilities are just as valid, and can be just as debilitating, as those that are more visibly recognized. As instructors, we are bound to encounter students who live with at least one invisible disability and it is our responsibility to help ensure that we provide an inclusive and accessible atmosphere for these students to the best of our abilities. Awareness, understanding, empathy and flexibility are the keys to providing an optimal learning environment for our students with unseen disabilities.

Elizabeth Sierra-Zarella studies and teaches in the Department of Child and Family Studies at Syracuse University.

Informational Links

http://www.invisibledisabilities.com: The Invisible Disabilities Advocate Web site. Includes chapter 1 of *But You Look Good! Why Seeing Is Not Believing with Chronic Illness and Pain* and *Disabled? You Don't LOOK Disabled: Unmasking Society's Depiction of People With Disabilities.*

http://www.theacpa.org/whatispain.htm: The American Chronic Pain Association.

http://www.niams.nih.gov/hi/topics/vitiligo/vitiligo.htm: A thorough question-and-answer article on vitiligo by the National Institute of Health.

http://www.vitiligofoundation.org/handbook.htm: Another great resource on vitiligo.

http://www.lungusa.org/site/pp.asp?c=dvLUK9O0E&b=33276: The American Lung Association's Asthma & Allergy page.

http://www.counseling.org/site/PageServer?pagename=consumers: The American Counseling Association's consumer site. Addresses mental health issues and provides consumer information about counseling practices.

"We're Not Stupid": My College Years as a Mentally Challenged Student

Anthony J. Nocella, II

This is the story of my educational career at a number of post-secondary academic institutions as a mentally challenged student. These experiences have led me to conclude that the higher education system in the classrooms, admissions offices, counselors' offices and registrars' offices is prejudiced against those with learning challenges and that the system encourages their segregation. There are laws for people with mental challenges, but those laws are unjust, are not always enforced and are too weak. It is my hope that my story will enlighten and inspire others to help make the changes that are necessary for people with learning challenges to succeed.

The story begins

Like many other mentally challenged students, I found that entering and being part of higher education was difficult, and sometimes, a very depressing experience. It is for this reason that I decided to tell my story. Note, that I do not explain what my "mental challenge" is in any great detail. I avoided this for a number of reasons: first, and most importantly, to allow others who fall under this large umbrella (mentally challenged) to relate better to my experience; second, because I believe this experience should not be so narrowly focused, especially if my goal is to speak to and encourage an array of people with "disabilities": and third, because I have a number of diagnoses, which include manic depression, dis-phonic, reading disabled, writing disabled, visually disabled, obsessive-compulsive disorder and attention deficit hyperactivity disorder. I do not believe that discussing these in detail is necessary for my purpose. It is important to note that the combination of these disabilities contributed to the conclusion by many psychiatrists that I would never graduate high school, let alone college. I do want to be clear that I did not avoid detailed references of my specific challenges because I am ashamed or embarrassed; I am neither. While my challenges are invisible and I have the choice to tell others what they are, I never shy away from telling people about them if issues needs to be addressed. I am proud of who I am as everyone with "disabilities" should be. Further, I have found that my "disabilities" are my advantages. For instance, because I am hyper ("energetic"), I want and need only five hours of sleep a night. Thus, I am able to work more. Because I have obsessive-compulsive disorder, I am naturally organized. I am also well-known for being able to multi-task on a large scale, be it working on a few books at a time or organizing conferences.

Preparing to attend college

During my senior year in high school—a private school for students with learning challenges[1]—I received a reality check from my family, friends and teachers; I needed to figure out what I was going to do after I graduated. Because of social pressure, I decided to attend college. The question was whether I could make it.

My only other option was to work somewhere that did not require a college degree and did not require much reading. However, I was unsure what to study. Because of my mental challenges, I am not someone who can attend college as an undeclared major; I literally panic when I do not have structure or my life plan mapped out. I needed structure and, more

---

[1] I attended the school for mentally challenged students from fourth grade on.

importantly, control. After looking at all the possible majors, I decided on forestry.[2]

My high school counselor and I began to look at all of the great options of universities to attend, only to find out that I could not be accepted if I did not have the required grade-point average or SAT score. My SAT score was 720—pretty low. This really shut a lot of doors for me, despite the fact that I had attended a private school for mentally challenged students, where I had two one-on-one classes everyday with a teacher for grammar and writing. The other classes were no larger than twelve students, but most had about four students. In this setting, I was given a lot of specialized attention. Each teacher knew my needs and met with my parents at least once a month to reflect on my progress and difficulties; further, this school not only provided students s pecialized attention, but did not grade using a standardized methodology. While each student was graded on class test scores, there was much more emphasis on the student's individual progress. I did not realize how much this school aided me until I graduated and went off to college.

After a long search for a college, I found one that had an excellent forestry program, one of the best in the country. The school (12,000 pop.) had a different set of criteria than other universities. It stated that if students fell into a certain percentile in their classes, they would be accepted with no SAT score requirement.

Well, that was it. I had found my way into higher education. I was accepted and went. Everyone was so happy for me— my counselor, family, teachers, principal, advisors and friends. It is important to note that only few individuals through the history of my high school have journeyed to "large"[3] four-year schools.

---

[2] Before my undergraduate career was complete, I changed my major from geology to art history to environmental science, only to graduate with a BA in political science.

[3] A student population over 4,000.

Most graduates take blue-collar jobs, work for family businesses,[4] or attend a small liberal arts school that provides extra attention for students with mental challenges. Further, because of my severe mental challenges I was not even expected to graduate high school.

College number one

When I attended this large public university, I soon realized I was lost, overwhelmed and quickly labeled by professors as "lazy and not smart." Representatives from the forestry program indicated to me that I was the first student they'd had who was documented with learning disabilities and had requested assistance. (I most likely was the first who requested assistance, but I am sure I was not the first one who was documented having a "learning disability.") They did not know what to do or how to assist me. Thus, they did not help me more than was legally expected, under the American Disabilities Act. I was literally a test subject for their administration's office. I was pulled out of class to take tests, I was ordered to sit in the front, and I was provided a note taker, all with little sensitivity or privacy. I was so embarrassed. Professors had no knowledge of my needs; thus, they were highly crass.

The first time I had to have the professors sign all of my disability forms, I experienced a horrible conversation. When I asked my botany professor to sign my disability form, he replied, "If Helen Keller can do it, than you can too." At the end of a very much insulting conversation he signed my forms and said, "Good luck," in a sarcastic tone. At once, I dropped the class and reported the conversation to disability services. I could not believe that he would group all people with "disabilities" together; it was pure prejudice. I, being white and coming from an upper-class family,

---

[4] Because my school was private, it was only available to a few people for scholarships, but the rest were people that could afford the tuition, which meant that a high percent of people were upper class.

had never experienced prejudice that direct before. It pierced me, to the point that I still think of that experience every time I have to tell someone I am mentally challenged. It was then when I found I could relate to people who have been excluded and insulted because of something they cannot change about themselves (e.g., being gay, race, sex, age, or physically challenged). That professor's comment was as prejudiced as someone saying to a visually challenged individual who wants to learn the piano; they should be as good as Stevie Wonder or Ray Charles. If I told a high school basketball player that he or she should be able to slam-dunk a basketball because Michael Jordan could in high school, he or she would laugh at me and most likely say, "Yeah, that was Jordan." I guess I should have said, "Yeah, that was Keller."

The forestry department had an unspoken system in which they "weeded out" students who were lazy. But, what about someone like me who attended the same class four times a week even though it was required only once; met the instructors once a week for one-on-one conferences; and studied every moment of the day? I failed all of my classes except jogging. I was being weeded out.

By the next semester, I got the system down, and I worked twice as hard. I passed with four Bs and one A. However, I had had enough of that program and the university, so I left.

College number two

My next experience was at a community college. I attended that college until I found a four year university that would better suit my needs. In this admissions process, I was fearful because I had to show everyone—professors, counselors and registrar officials (who were students my own age)—my GPA and my SAT score. Also, I had to prove that I had a "learning disability." The hoops I had to jump through were ridiculous. I spent at least 20-plus hours the first week of class just working with my counselor and admissions to tell the faculty I needed "special help."

Emotional torture is the only way to describe it. I had meeting after meeting with the same counselor to get help explaining how to register for classes as well as to provide her the official documentation of my mental disabilities. The rest of the process included registering for my classes, going back to my counselor, the counselor sending a letter to all of my professors, picking up the letter from each professor and giving it back to her. This was all in addition to meeting with each of my professors to explain my needs. This was a very inefficient and unfair process that is prejudiced against students with mental challenges.

College number three

The university where I finally earned my BA in political science was a positive experience for the most part. Of course, there was a philosophy professor who pulled me aside to talk to me about my grades. I said to him, "I understand the information and even tutor other students in class, but I cannot write it down because of my learning disabilities." I have never forgotten what he said in reply: "Everyone has learning disabilities. You just need to deal with it." I told the dean of student affairs, but because of the professor's international academic status and tenure, nothing could be done. However, I must also note that because of the small size of the private university, I was given a lot of attention, and faculty focused more on the students than on research, which was not the case at the first university I attended. I had a number of professors who took time out of their personal schedules to read with me, look over my notes and edit my papers before they were due. These professors were outstanding and they gave me the attention I needed to succeed.

College number four

My next college experience was in pursuit of my master's degree. I did not have the minimum grades (2.96) or the GRE score (I did not take it) to get into most graduate programs. That, I think was the largest obstacle pursuing my master's. Most master's programs look at the undergraduate school of prospective students (e.g., Ivy League), their GPA and their GRE scores—all standards that would work against me. The only way that I was going to be accepted into a program was to personally introduce myself and inform them of my many unique experiences. I could not prove myself on paper or by test results. Thus, I avoided such measures and looked for alternatives.

I had to find a university that did not require the GRE and provided another means to be accepted. To further complicate the matter, I knew I would be paying my own tuition. When I looked into scholarships and loans, I found that scholarships went to students who had the required GPA scores, and loans went to students who were already accepted. I was a student with a low GPA and no GRE. I finally found a small liberal arts school in California that under certain conditions would accept me. I was so excited.

However, I was accepted into the university under the status of *unclassified standing*. The requirements of that standing were that I had to achieve a certain GPA to be officially accepted (no grades under a B). Hence, not being officially accepted, I could not obtain any loans. In applying to this university, I also had to ask my undergraduate professors to write about my learning challenges, about whether I was a knowledgeable and hard working student and whether I should be accepted into the university.

This school was the most unprepared and unequipped for students with learning disabilities of all the schools I attended. They had *no* official counselor for students with disabilities; students were routed to the dean of student affairs. I must say, the dean tried his hardest, but he still lacked the skills needed for the job. If I had not been familiar with the admissions process and what I could legally ask for, I most likely would not gotten much help. I actually had to create a form, so I could document my needs and my disabilities for admissions, faculty and staff. This form is still being used to this day for all students with learning challenges at that school. I was amazed that they did not have anything in place, not even the legal forms that I believed they were required by law to have.

The best part of my experience at this university was the teaching approach in my specific program (peacemaking and conflict studies). They taught in the Oxford style, which allowed students to have classes with professors privately. In my opinion this is the finest way for a student to succeed in education.

College number five

Today, after many personal long phone calls with the chair of my department and faculty asking whether I can read, write, edit, etc., a long narrative (which was part of my application) and five recommendations (including one from my high school, only three were required), I am a student at Syracuse University, where I am currently working on my doctorate in Social Science. I must admit that if Dr. Robert Bogdan, who is an advocate and is knowledgeable about learning challenges and "disabilities," had not been the chair of the department, I most likely would not have been accepted. Not that I am under-qualified, but when I inform most professors that I have learning challenges, they think of me as a second-rate student. I then have to tell them my experiences and show them my curriculum vita, which includes a number of articles that I have written, a published manual, and a published book I co-edited. Generally speaking, professors think people with learning challenges are helpless. They tend to speak slower, louder and ask repetitively, "Do you understand?" They speak down to us, in the way one would speak to a baby or puppy. We're not stupid; we're different. It is for this reason that I *stress* the importance of having a more diverse faculty at all universities that includes faculty with physical and mental challenges who can be advocates for people with physical and mental challenges.

Conclusion

As I began recently to speak out more about my learning challenges, I began to demand more. Professors told me repetitively throughout my educational career, "You are just not as knowledgeable as most students." Well, yes I was. I am, just not as knowledgeable in the method in which they have the advantage.

Through the troubles and prejudices of my higher educational experiences, I found that universities and colleges must be changed to aid mentally challenged students. Among the necessary changes are waivers of standardized testing, waivers of GPAs and the elimination of the standard writing samples as a consideration for acceptance. Instead, applicants should be asked a set of questions in an interview format that are formulated by a university committee made up of representatives from admissions, the faculty, the president's office, the dean's office, the counseling staff and the chancellor's office. For the first two semesters, classes should be chosen by faculty in accordance with the students' chosen workload. With no minimum or maximum workload, students would automatically be listed as a full-time student. If students make it through the first year, they could then choose their own classes. Universities should also require personal orientations on campus with counselors before school starts. This would involve walking students all over campus, introducing them to their professors and figuring out their daily activities (e.g., where to get food, rest and how to figure out transportation). These suggestions are just the beginning of the changes that should come, but the current process of "dealing" with mentally challenged students must be challenged and new methods must be adopted in all universities and colleges.

The steps to create a fairer educational system begins with an awareness campaign, with people knowing the difference between those who are lazy and those who have learning challenges. Next, we must educate staff and faculty about how to constructively assist people with learning challenges. Finally, students with mental challenges must voi eir concerns and stop hiding the fact they need help and are different. They need to first convince themselves that they are not "stupid"; I think that was my hardest battle—coming to an understanding of what diversity truly means.

Anthony J. Nocella, II, is a Social Science doctoral student in the Maxwell School at Syracuse University.

Crucial Communication Triangle: Students with Disabilities, Faculty and Disability Support Services

Sara Pace

As a new instructor of English composition in the fall of 1999, I walked into class my first day already assuming that there would be surprises and new challenges. I had read past and current teaching theory for composition and felt confident that I could lead a class through a semester-long series of papers, discussions and readings. One thing that had *not* been discussed in much depth in my graduate courses, however, was how to act as a liaison between students with disabilities and administrators of the services designed to support them. I attribute this lack of attention to disability to the assumption that problems such as those I encountered in my classes are unlikely to occur in universities and colleges. But what I learned my first year of teaching shaped me more as a teacher and as an advocate of disability issues than any other experience in the five years I've taught since then. Essentially, what I learned is that open communication is key to access.

Experience has taught me that faculty, staff and graduate teaching assistants must take active roles in making sure that students with disabilities receive appropriate access/accommodations. Taking on such a role also assumes the ability on the part of instructors to take risks in supplementing the role of the Disability Support Services office (DSS) on their campuses.

Because DSS offices are not necessarily aware of how our individual pedagogies may create barriers for students with disabilities, we have to develop this awareness ourselves. We must build a level of trust with our students so that we can effectively confront issues of access when they arise. My blueprint for ways in which instructors can become more involved in accomodations and maintain good lines of communication with students and the DSS office comes from my experiences during the 1999-2000 academic year.

　　　　The situation that helped me evolve as a teacher involved a student with a hearing disability who was in my first-year composition class. The DSS office provided her with a sign interpreter at the start of the semester. The interpreter, however, generally either did not show up to class, or showed up late and, literally, with a hangover. (He was, by the way, assigned to sign with her in *all* of her classes, so his absences had far-reaching consequences in each of her courses.) Even though the signer was clearly not helpful or always present *in* class, the student at first felt the need to turn to him *outside* of class for clarification on assignments. I've since reasoned that early on, she, both as a new student and a student with a disability, may have felt intimidated and reluctant to approach her instructors about feeling out of the loop. The signer, since he lived in the dorms, probably seemed more accessible. However, after my feedback on her first paper revealed that his interpretation of the assignment criteria was way off-base, the student began to assert herself in seeking clarification and feedback from me directly. She became much more open and comfortable about sharing her frustrations with access and her questions about her progress in the class. At this point, our collaborative odyssey to make sure the student had proper access began. Here are some ways in which we made the semester go a little more smoothly:

One-On-One Meetings

　　　　First, the student and I found different ways to

communicate about the course content and her writing that helped to make her classroom experience more bearable and successful. She came to see me (sans interpreter of course; if it was the difficult for him to make his appointed schedule, he certainly was not going to appear for out-of-class conferences) in my office several times so that we could discuss assignments one-on-one. Although nearly deaf since birth, she was a magnificent lip reader, a very fortunate skill considering the circumstances. Because she was such a skilled lip reader, these discussions were productive for her. We developed a great rapport outside of the classroom, which must have seemed an intimidating and oppressive environment for her because of the lack of access through a competent signer.

Technology for Communication

Often, we also conversed through e-mail to clarify class concepts that she might have missed. E-mail is a powerful tool for communication between instructors and students, and this student quickly mastered the art of shooting me a note when she was confused about something said in class or when she needed to let me know that the signer had failed to perform his duties. I noticed that she appeared a little more comfortable discussing things in this milieu, and so I would encourage other instructors to be as open to e-mail communication as they are to face-to-face meetings. Students, especially those who have mobility-related disabilities, need to know that we are accessible through technology and not just during office hours.

Providing Lecture Notes

I also provided her with a separate set of lecture notes and concepts daily to help her follow along. Many professors and instructors, I know, are squeamish about providing any student with lecture notes. However, the extremeness of this particular situation told me intuitively that this was the right thing to do.

The student expressed her appreciation for the notes and felt that they helped her follow along. Seeing the notes in writing not only gave her the information she needed, but it also let her in on the cues for stopping places for discussion and class activities. I did this also for another student that semester who had visual and hearing disabilities. In his case, he also found it helpful to copy the notes of other classmates. After that semester, I was asked to do the same for a student with a hearing disability in a literature course at my new institution. Doing so worked well again, especially since this student had a diligent signer who used the notes as a signing aid.

Though my composition student and I used makeshift measures to see that she got the information she needed, I was horrified and embarrassed for her. I was also upset that I was incapable of finding a quick fix to the signer's antics. I attempted to make face-to-face, phone and e-mail contact with the DSS director about the signer's absences and incompetence throughout the term, but direct contact with him proved difficult. He did, however, respond to my supervisor (our writing program administrator), who called the DSS director when I alerted him to the signer's incompetence. The information the DSS director provided us with concerning the situation was disheartening, but it greatly helped me understand what I needed to do for the student. We were both shocked to learn from the DSS administrator that this signer, in fact, had a *history* of such behavior, and that somehow it was decided that transferring him to a new college might remedy his problem. Thankfully, the DSS director promised to talk with both the signer and the student.

As her instructor, I appreciated the gesture, but unfortunately the communication that took place among them did little to remedy the situation. I was dumbfounded. Here was a perfectly good, hardworking student with her grades already in jeopardy due to faulty accommodations. Her access to lecture notes, facility in participating in class discussions and activities, and comfort level with the course itself had all been compromised by the signer's absence and apathy (as well as, I have to admit, my own lack of preparedness in confronting situations such as this). Even so, she and I made it work by communicating outside of the classroom through meetings, e-mail and lecture notes.

As the semester wore on, the student began to confide in me about her anger and disappointment toward the interpreter; she even said she was considering transferring to another institution. I told her at one point after class that, were it up to me, I would dismiss the signer and find a new one. This was possibly an unprofessional move for someone in her first semester of teaching, but it was one I felt was necessary, given my inability to do what so clearly needed to be done in hiring a good signer.

Of course, our obligation to advocate for and with our students should not end when the semester is over. After the term ended, I was surprised to find out from the student that this same signer would return to work with her the next semester. I wrote a final e-mail to the director arguing that bringing this signer back would directly harm the student's ability to participate in her courses (as it had done in my class in the beginning). Although I did not receive a reply, the signer was replaced before the next term and, to my knowledge, the student had an A average in her second-semester composition course at midterm. I would like to believe that my final communication with the DSS office in some way prompted the decision to find another interpreter.

This example is the most complex situation I have encountered in working with students toward acceptable access in terms of the amount of outside work the student and I engaged in to make sure she could successfully complete the course. At the end of the semester she thanked me for my help, but it was she who had taken the initiative to point out when she needed something. And my communication with the DSS office (though limited) helped greatly in realizing just how proactive I needed to be in this situation. I learned that that we should not hesitate to work outside of class with our students with disabilities to make sure they get proper access to our teaching. We may not always be quick to realize when a lecture style, the use of a particular technology or a certain class activity may hamper a student's participation in a course. So it is important to allow students access to *ourselves* as well.

As instructors, our involvement in the accommodation of and access for our students with disabilities must go beyond pasting in the college's disability services statement into our syllabi and assuming our students and the DSS offices will be able to work everything out from there. I have only experiential knowledge, but I do have some ideas for maintaining the communication triangle.

First, we should develop a level of trust with students so they feel comfortable coming to us if needs are not being met. Let them know how we feel about unmet needs. Even if we are unable to completely remedy a situation, as in this case, knowing that we are on their side can go a long way in developing a strong rapport. Secondly, we should experiment with media, especially e-mail or real time conferencing spaces, that both students and instructors have access to in discussing assignments and concepts. Thirdly, it is crucial to maintain communication with the students *and*, whenever possible, with the DSS staff. We should find out and get to know who is running the DSS office and who we can go to when things seem to go awry. We should ask questions if we are not sure whether we are providing appropriate access. If possible, we should ask our own supervisors to get involved with the DSS office if we have trouble making contact. The frequent lack of communication between myself and the DSS office led to some flying-by-the-seat-of-our-pants accomodations that I am sure made it uncomfortable for this student at times. Even though we may try our best, we cannot always recreate many necessary accommodations that the DSS offices are generally more skilled in providing.

It is my hope that my particular experiences can be a wake-up call for all of us to acknowledge how we can positively shape the experiences of our students with disabilities. New and experienced instructors should not necessarily rely on all DSS entities to take care of all access issues. Many times we have to step in, and, through our collaborative ingenuity with our students with disabilities *and* DSS staff, shift our practices to fill in gaps. When we are fortunate enough to have efficient and caring Disability Support Services staff and administrators, we *must* maintain communication with them so that our students are given the access they need to succeed.

Sara Pace teaches English at Texas Woman's University

Signs of Inclusion: Using Sign Language Interpreters in the Classroom

Jeremy L. Brunson

The composition of the classroom has changed over the last few decades. In some cases, it now includes a third party who provides a visual rendition of the auditory information occurring in the classroom: a Sign Language interpreter. I have worked as a Sign Language interpreter in a variety of settings for more than nine years. Each of these settings has unique challenges, and working in an educational setting is no different. The dynamic that exists among the interpreter, the student and the instructor can be a complicated one; success requires that instructors do more than simply make space available for an interpreter near the front of the class. Awareness and cooperation on the part of the instructor are essential.

Three aspects of such awareness and cooperation are especially important to the successful relationship: clear communication about the instructor's expectations of the interpreter, modifications to lecturing styles, and scheduling considerations for events outside the classroom.

This, or any text, is not a substitute for face-to-face interaction. To have a truly inclusive learning and teaching experience, instructors should first consult with deaf [1] students enrolled in the class. Establishing a meeting with deaf students the first week of class is key to understanding their needs and how best to accommodate them.

There are a variety of communication modes used by deaf people. Some deaf individuals who are fluent in English, but are unable to hear may prefer a method called Cued Speech. This modality uses different hand shapes that represent various sounds. This is not a language. It is a visual representation of spoken English. Another method called Signing Exact English, commonly referred to as SEE, is a hybrid of American Sign Language and visual cues (not Cued Speech) to convey messages visually. Similar to Cued Speech, this is not a recognized language. Although instructors may see these two methods used in their classrooms, I will not focus those modalities in this essay. Instead, I will focus on the use of American Sign Language, which is the dominant language used by deaf people in America and parts of Canada. American Sign Language has its own syntax and grammar (Lane, 1999). Once instructors have a broader understanding of the processes involved when working between an auditory language and a visual language, it is my hope that they will be able to adjust their teaching styles to accommodate other communication modalities.

Working with the Interpreter

It is becoming more common to see sign language interpreters in classrooms as an accommodation. Interpreters work for everyone in the classroom. When they are present, it is because at least two people who have something to say to one another do not share a common language. Sign language interpreters are trained to assist in this interaction, but they do not necessarily have training in education. Although the interpreter might hold a degree in the subject that she or he is interpreting, the role of the interpreter is as an interpreter, not an instructor.

---

[1] Although it is customary to use "person first" language when discussing individuals who are labeled disabled (i.e., person with a mental retardation), most people who use American Sign Language see themselves as members of a cultural minority and, therefore, often place their cultural marker first (i.e., deaf person, African American).

Therefore, students and instructors should recognize that interpreters are not tutors and are not substitutes for interaction with the instructor. Interpreters are hired because they are skilled in two languages and two cultures, and are able to interpret between them (Neumann Solow, 2000).

To learn how to work together, interpreters and instructors should meet. Although it is ideal, instructors and interpreters do not always have the opportunity to discuss the logistics of working together before the first day of class. This is because of the limited time availability of both the instructor and the interpreter. Interpreters who are university employees are generally able to meet with instructors outside of class, and can document this time as part of their work hours. However, not every university has staff interpreters. Interpreters who are "freelance," or not employed by the university, may not be able to seek remuneration for the time spent preparing for the class and, therefore, may forego any formal meetings with the instructor outside of the scheduled class. Often interpreters will arrive on the day of the first class and attempt to meet with instructors at some point. This is the time when interpreters can introduce themselves and discuss their roles in the classroom.

Often the interpreters and instructors need only meet once to discuss the logistics of working together. With the exception of situations in which an interpreter must be absent from a class, it is traditional that the same interpreter work in the same class throughout the semester. Since interpreters are assigned for entire semesters, they tend to build rapport with the instructors. This also allows interpreters to build a knowledge base of class material as the semester progresses. Over time, interpreters become familiar with the teaching styles of the instructors and with the course materials; thus, the interpreters become more effective.

The interpreting process

Regardless of how familiar interpreters become with the

teaching styles of instructors, there will be times when interpreters might have to interrupt the lecture. This might occur because the pace of the lecture is too quick. Clarification helps interpreters provide accurate interpretations for students. Interpreters vary on how they interrupt instructors. Most often, interpreters do not raise their hands and wait to for the instructor to acknowledge them. They might just simply ask, "Excuse me, could you slow down?" Although this may seem like a personal affront, instructors must realize that interpreters must ensure that deaf students do not miss any information. Instructors and interpreters should discuss how to handle such interruptions at the beginning of the semester.

Another time that is awkward for instructors is when interpreters convey the ideas of deaf students. When conveying such comments, interpreters speak in first-person. For example, when deaf students comment or have questions, interpreters say "I" instead of "he" or "she." Using the first-person removes the interpreter from the interaction. However, it can be understandably confusing to non-signing people. Misunderstandings might arise because the non-signing person is unclear about who is actually speaking. When interpreters need clarification some are now beginning to say, "The interpreter would like to know." or "The interpreter has a question." In the absence of statements that directly refer to the interpreter, it should be assumed that the deaf student is making the inquiry. Of course, if any confusion exists, instructors should ask for clarification. Once again, interpreters and instructors should negotiate these logistical issues at the beginning of the semester.

One area that is not negotiable is the actual work of the interpreter. There is no verbatim translation from English to American Sign Language. Therefore, it is sometimes necessary for interpreters to wait until instructors complete thoughts before they begin to provide their interpretations. Often instructors become concerned when they are talking and interpreters do not seem to be signing. However, the job of interpreting is not only visual. A great deal of the work of interpreting is invisible, but no less important. Although this process of pausing for the instructor's full idea allows for greater understanding and improved accuracy in the interpreting process (Cokely, 1986), it also delays the rendering of information.

The product of this delay often creates a situation in which deaf students receive information several seconds after the other students. Couple the interpreting process with the students' internal processing of the information, and minutes could lapse before they are ready to participate in any discussion. Instructors have a lot of information that they are providing during a class. The pace is often quick and instructors may move from one topic to the next quickly. Therefore, the comments and questions of deaf students might seem out of place. In reality, they have just received and considered the information that the rest of the class received minutes before.

This is also true when an interpreter is working from American Sign Language to English. This can be the most uncomfortable time for non-signers because, in U.S. English speaking culture, silence is uncomfortable. Often, when people are signing, interpreters must wait until they are near completion of their comments before they are able to begin translating into English. This is for accuracy purposes. However, non-signing individuals such as instructors and classmates often become impatient and are curious as to why students are signing, but interpreters are not speaking. Rest assured that this is part of the process. The two languages are not interchangeable and interpreters must work to provide non-signers with comprehendible interpretations. It should be mentioned, however, that there are exceptions. There are some deaf people who are fluent in English and, therefore, the process may require less time. Instructors must trust that interpreters are skilled, and in most cases credentialed, to effectively do the job of interpreting. This means that interpreters understand the amount of time they need before providing visual or auditory renditions of messages.

Credentials

North American society places a lot of importance on credentials, especially for those individuals who work in an academic setting. American Sign Language interpreters are no exception. Two national credentials are relevant to the discussion of interpreters: the Certification of Interpreting and the Certification of Transliteration. Holders of the Certification of Interpretation are qualified to interpret between American Sign Language and English. Holders of the Certification of Transliteration are qualified to interpret between spoken English and an English-based sign system. The Registry of Interpreters for the Deaf grants these certifications after an interpreter has successfully passed a series of tests (see Neumann Solow, 2000; Stewart, Schein and Cartwright, 1998; and Frishberg, 1990). The holders of these certifications are "credentialed" to provide communication access.

Instructors must understand that these are not teaching credentials; interpreters are not responsible for the learning of deaf students and the same rules that protect the privacy of all students apply. Instructors might be tempted to ask interpreters whether students are learning the material or keeping up with the class. These questions are for the students, not for the interpreters. There are times when interpreters might want to address certain issues with the instructors about how the class is progressing. These questions should involve only their work as interpreters. Any discussions of a student's abilities, progress in classes or grades are inappropriate unless the student is present, and is an active participant in the conversations.

The same considerations apply to classes with labs. Often instructors assume that interpreters will work with deaf students in labs or act as educational aids. In some cases, it might seem more convenient for interpreters to assume this role; however, doing this hampers the learning opportunities of deaf students. Part of the educational experience is interacting with one's peers. If interpreters assume the role of lab partners, they segregate the students from the rest of the class.

Lecturing styles

Small modifications or considerations in the lecturing styles of instructors can aid interpreters in their work. The suggestions that follow require minimum alterations to teaching styles, but will likely have considerable impact of the efficiency and efficacy of the work of interpreters.

Class notes

Although interpreters are hired to facilitate communication between parties, it is always helpful to have agendas and notes of lectures. The goal of interpreters is to provide messages, including intent and appropriate emphasis, to the people for whom they are interpreting (Cokely, 1992). To be effective, it is beneficial for instructors to provide "road maps" marked with key points that they hope their audiences will absorb from the interactions. Different interpreters handle this in different ways. The most common way interpreters address this issue is by asking instructors for the notes for the classes, any required texts, and time to discuss any new concepts. Most instructors are extremely busy and might forget to make extra copies of their notes ahead of time. If possible, the notes for the following week should be given to interpreters on the Friday before. This allows interpreters ample time to read the notes and become familiar with the readings. Syllabi are helpful; however, there are times when instructors discuss items not covered on the syllabus during class. It is much easier for interpreters to be prepared for the class if instructors can provide interpreters with the notes they will follow that day. Providing interpreters with class notes is easier now with the advent of new technology and its use in the classroom.

Technology in the classroom

The methods used for teaching have changed with the advancement of technology. One change is that more instructors are using Power Point in the classroom. Not only is this beneficial to the students in the class, but it also makes it easier for instructors to print out copies of presentations for interpreters. In some cases, instructors might want to send Power Points as attachments to the interpreters via email.

Computer programs are not the only type of technology being used in classrooms; movies have been used for decades. However, it is worth discussing the effect of movies in classrooms when working with interpreters. It is important that instructors first check to see whether movies are closed-captioned. This is the subtitle at the bottom of the screen. Older movies might not have that capability. Most videos that have closed-captions have a "CC" on the box or videotape case. Although there are other markers that denote closed-captions, the "CC" is the most common. When in doubt, instructors should consult deaf students or the Disability Resource Center. Due to legislation by the Federal Communications Commission, televisions produced after 1993 are equipped with closed-captioning chips. If classrooms have older televisions or LCD projectors and instructors wish to show movies, instructors should also make sure that decoders are available. Instructors should contact the Disability Resource Center or the facilities department on their campuses for this information.

A sign language interpreter is not a substitute for captioned programs. Even the most skilled interpreter would have difficulty accurately interpreting an entire movie and successfully conveying a character (tone, attitude, belief etc.) in her or his entirety. For example, imagine the challenge of providing the dynamics of the characters in *12 Angry Men.* Not only does the deaf student have to focus solely on the interpreter, missing key visual components of the movie, but the interpreter may not be able to keep up with the pace of the dialogue. Captioning allows students to focus in one direction and move quickly from line 21 (where the captioning appears) and back to the movie.

This or that

Understanding the capability of the technology in the classroom is one way instructors can assist interpreters in doing their jobs. Another way is by the words instructors choose to use. It is common practice for instructors to use terms such as "this" or "that" while pointing to something on the board. This is particularly difficult for interpreters. Interpreters often sit with their backs to the blackboard. When instructors point to something without identifying it, interpreters must turn to see what is being discussed to properly interpret it. In some classes, such as mathematics, it is more acceptable to use less precise terms because a great deal of the lecture is being written on the board simultaneously and all students are copying down the equation. In these classes, interpreters are able to direct the attention of students to the board. However, when the class is lecture style, interpreters are at a loss without seeing what "this" or "that" is.

To avoid these types of problems, instructors should be mindful of their speaking habits and should make an earnest effort to identify what they are talking about rather than using vague words like "this" or "that." This is beneficial for all students in the classroom. This allows those students who are taking notes to follow the discussion much easier and interpreters are able to provide more accurate interpretations.

Scheduling Issues

I would now like to focus on issue of scheduling outside events. Learning is not confined to classrooms; instructors are increasingly providing opportunities to earn extra credit for students who are willing to go to events outside the classroom. This can create dilemmas for students who use the services of sign language interpreters. Most interpreters schedule their work at least five days in advance. If students would like to attend out-of-class events, the information should be provided at the beginning of the semester so that they can schedule interpreters.

In the event that outside exercises are required, instructors should consult with deaf students and interpreters to determine how they can be handled. The interpreters who work with the students in class might not be available for particular events. Deaf students might need to contact the campus Disability Resource Center or local interpreter referral agencies to schedule interpreters. Again, it is important that enough notification is provided to students so that they are able to arrange for the accommodations they need.

Some types of events, such as plays, are difficult to interpret. Many interpreters may want notice several months in advance, so they are able to rehearse and see the play several times. Substitute assignments may be necessary if the student is unable to secure an interpreter for a particular event. However, it should never be assumed that the deaf students would rather have an alternative assignment than see the play. Again, discussion with deaf students is critical.

Conclusion

Let me back up for a moment and consider how to get interpreters and under what circumstances they are needed. Deaf students often inform instructors if they need the services of interpreters, and the logistics of getting interpreters usually occur before the first day of classes. For meetings outside of classes, such as office hours, instructors should consult with deaf students about the need for interpreters. Students might sometimes feel comfortable communicating by using notes or reading lips. However, interpreters are not provided only for the sake of the students. If instructors feel they are unable to communicate effectively without interpreters, they should request the accommodation of a Sign Language interpreter.

To hire interpreters, instructors can consult with deaf students or they can contact the Disability Resource Center of the campus. Consulting the student is preferable. Deaf students are most familiar with their own accommodation needs and might have interpreters they prefer. Additionally, discussing the issues of accommodation with all of the parties affected by the presence or absence of a sign language interpreter improves the chances that each party's needs are met.

Finally, instructors should remember that working between two languages and providing accurate interpretations of any subject matter is a difficult task. Most important for the educational success of deaf students is that constant communication among the deaf student, interpreter and the instructor always exist. These three individuals must always work together, as a team.

Jeremy L. Brunson is a sign language interpreter and a graduate student in Sociology and Disability Studies at Syracuse University.

References

Cokely, D. (1986). The effects of lag time on interpreter errors. *Sign Language Studies*, 53: 341-376.

Cokely, D. (1992). *Interpretation: A sociolinguistic model.* Linstock Press: Burtonsville, MD.

Frishberg, N. (1990). *Interpreting: An introduction* (rev. ed.). RID Publications: Silver Springs, M.D.

Hoemann, H.W. (1986). *Introduction to American Sign Language.* Bowling Green Press, Inc.: Bowling Green, O.H.

Humphrey, J. H. and B. J. Alcorn. (1994). *So you want to be an interpreter: An introduction to sign language interpreting.* H & H Publishers: Amarillo, TX.

Lane, H. (1992). *The mask of benevolence: Disabling the Deaf community.* DawnSignPress, Inc.: San Diego, C.A.

Neumann Solow, S. (2000). *Sign language interpreting: A basic resource book* (rev. ed.). Linstock Press: Burtsonville, M.D.

Metzger, M. (1999). *Sign language interpreting: Deconstructing the myth of neutrality.* Gallaudet University Press: Washington, D.C.

Stewart, D.A., J. D. Schein, and B. E. Cartwright. (1998). *Sign language interpreting: Exploring its art and science.* Allyn and Bacon: Boston, M.A.

Legal Requirements for Students with Disabilities and Universities

Crystal Doody
Julie Morse

Discrimination against people with disabilities has led to the passage of federal laws designed to ensure equal protection of persons with disabilities in all areas of society. These federal laws help us move toward the goal of social inclusion and civil rights for everyone. Prior to 1973, disabled students were not provided with equal rights to access and accommodations in higher education.[i] Students with disabilities were excluded from colleges and universities because of inaccessible facilities and services. Although the Fourteenth Amendment guarantees equal protection, there was a lack of legislation that specifically remedied the discrimination, isolation and segregation of those with disabilities. This finally began to change with the passage of two acts: Section 504 of the Rehabilitation Act and The Americans with Disabilities Act.

Section 504 and the ADA

Section 504 of the Rehabilitation Act of 1973 and the Americans with Disabilities Act (ADA) of 1990 were enacted to prohibit discrimination against persons with disabilities. The acts require both private and public colleges and universities to follow proscribed regulations specifying the appropriate treatment of persons with disabilities, including accommodations that are required by law. Virtually all higher education institutions are governed by the two acts because they receive federal funds.[ii] Since the passage of the Rehabilitation Act and the ADA, some, but not all, barriers to equal education for students with disabilities have been eliminated. As a result, enrollment of students with disabilities has increased significantly.[iii] A closer examination of the two acts will provide us with information necessary to identify the schools' responsibilities in ensuring students' rights.

Section 504 of the Rehabilitation Act provides that:

> No otherwise qualified individual with a disability…shall, solely by reason of her or his disability, be excluded from the participation in, be denied the benefits of, or be subjected to discrimination under any program or activity receiving Federal financial assistance…[iv]

Title II of the ADA, which covers public universities, provides that:

> …no qualified individual with a disability shall, by reason of such disability, be excluded from participation in or be denied the benefits of the services, programs, or activities of a public entity, or be subjected to discrimination by any such entity.[v]

Title III of the ADA, which covers private universities, provides that:

> No individual shall be discriminated against on the basis of disability in the full and equal enjoyment of the goods, services, facilities, privileges, advantages or accommodations of any place of public accommodation by any person who owns, leases (or leases to), or operates a place of public accommodation.[vi]

Applying Section 504 and the ADA

The Rehabilitation Act and the ADA require postsecondary educational institutions to provide qualified students, faculty and staff with reasonable accommodations.[vii] "To be qualified for a post-secondary education program…, an individual with a disability must be able to competently perform in the program… with or without the provision of reasonable accommodations."[viii] While it is unclear precisely what constitutes reasonable accommodations, courts have provided some guidance in defining this phrase. If an accommodation imposes an undue administrative or financial burden on the postsecondary educational institution, or if it requires a fundamental alteration of the program, the accommodation is considered unreasonable.[ix] Because of the varied nature of academic institutions, courts make such determinations on a case-by-case basis. Additionally, educational institutions are not required to lower their academic standards and students who cannot maintain the academic standards, with or without the reasonable accommodations, do not fit the definition of a qualified student with a disability.[x]

How students receive accommodations

Students with disabilities in higher education must self-identify as disabled if they wish to receive reasonable accommodations in both academic, as well as non-academic, services and programs.[xi] In other words, it is the responsibility of the student, not the teaching assistants or faculty, to disclose a disability to the university and to request accommodations. In some instances, a student may choose, for a variety of reasons, not to disclose a disability or to request accommodations.

Once a student shares this information, the university may require them to provide documentation of disabilities before discussing specific accommodations.[xii] Students must obtain this evaluation at their own expense.[xiii] Additionally, the evaluation should be sufficiently comprehensive[xiv] and conducted within the last few years by a certified expert.[xv] This evaluation aids the university in determining appropriate services the student may wish to access.

Types of accommodations

After a student establishes that she or he has a disability, the university and the student work together to determine which accommodations are necessary to meet the student's needs. Because university officials may be unfamiliar with various types of accommodations, students should be encouraged to request accommodations they believe can meet their learning needs. Regulations for Title II and Title III of the ADA contain provisions similar to those regulations for Section 504 of the Rehabilitation Act, which suggest three areas of accommodations: modifications of academic requirements, adjustments to course examinations and the provision of auxiliary aids.[xvi] Academic modifications, for example, may take the form of increased time to complete degree requirements, altering course methods or substituting courses to fulfill degree requirements that will not fundamentally alter the degree program.[xvii] For example, teaching assistants may present lesson materials in both print and audio format, or may utilize a variety of teaching methods concurrently to help ensure all students can access their learning environments in manners that are conducive to their learning needs. Course exams should be conducted in a manner that tests the student's proficiency in the course, rather than one which highlights the student's impairment.[xviii] This may include increased time for testing, or providing testing in alternative formats (i.e., providing a student with a scribe to write exams as students speaks it, reading the questions to the student or providing a computer on which a student may take exams). Students may also require auxiliary aids. Both Section 504 regulations and ADA regulations list examples of aids or services students might be entitled to, such as:

"...taped texts, interpreters or other effective methods of making orally delivered materials available to students with hearing impairments, readers in libraries for students with visual impairments, classroom equipment adapted for use by students with manual impairments, and other similar services and actions. Recipients need not provide attendants, individually prescribed devices, readers for personal use or study, or other devices or services of a personal nature."[xix]

Additionally, ADA regulations suggest such aids as "Brailled or large print texts or qualified readers for individuals with visual impairments and learning disabilities, [as well as] "provision of the course through videotape, cassettes, or prepared notes."[xx]

These examples are merely illustrative, and not exhaustive of the types of accommodations schools may provide for students with disabilities. Students with disabilities may require different or additional accommodations than those highlighted here and universities should tailor accommodations to fit the needs of each particular student. This helps to ensure that students receive adjustments that allow them to effectively access the courses and examinations and that the university provides an effective and appropriate learning environments for all students.

Limitations on Accommodations for Students with Disabilities

Neither Section 504 of the Rehabilitation Act nor the ADA require a university to provide accommodations for students who impose a direct threat to the health and safety of other members of university communities, or to themselves.[xxi] However, a college should be cautious that such ideas about health and safety are not based on paternalistic or maternalistic misconceptions about particular disabilities or generalized stereotypes about the capabilities of people with disabilities.[xxii] Instead, individualized, fact-specific inquires about each student aid a university in establishing whether a student might pose such a threat. The university should also consider whether reasonable modifications of policies, practices and procedures can mitigate the risk for the student and others.[xxiii] While not all students will be qualified to attend a certain college or university, schools must work to ensure that all students are evaluated based on their abilities and not devalued on the basis of their disability.

Conclusion

Section 504 and the ADA require colleges and universities to follow minimum standards for accommodation and access for disabled students. While this has increased access to post-secondary education for many students with disabilities, these standards should be only the starting point. All educators should consider how to move beyond mere compliance with the laws to create inclusive, educational environments for all students. Moving beyond compliance provides all students with richer learning environments that promote participation and acceptance.

Crystal Doody is a third year joint degree student in Law and Disability Studies and a founding member of the disAbility Law Society at Syracuse University.

Julie Morse is a third year joint degree student in Law and Disability Studies and a founding member of the disAbility Law Society at Syracuse University.

[i] Cloud, R. (2000). Higher Education Accommodations for Disabled Students, *West's Education Law Reporter*, 147, 391.

[ii] Id at 391.

[iii] Id at 391.

[iv] 29 U.S.C.A. § 794(a) (2004).

[v] 42 U.S.C.A. § 12132 (2004).

[vi] 42 U.S.C.A. § 12182(a) (2004).

[vii] Tucker, B. (1998). Disability Discrimination in Higher Education: A review of the 1997 judicial decisions. *The Journal of College and University Law*, 25, 353.

[viii] Id at 353.

[ix] Id at 354.

[x] Id at 354.

[xi] Tucker, B. (1996). Application of the Americans with Disabilities Act (ADA) and Section 504 to Colleges and Universities: An Overview and Discussion of Special Issues Relating to Students. *The Journal of College and University Law*, 23, 13.

[xii] Id. at 13.

[xiii] Id. at 14.

[xiv] Id. at 14.

[xv] Id. at 14.

[xvi] 34 C.F.R. § 104.44 (2004).

[xvii] 34 C.F.R. § 104.44(a) (2004).

[xviii] 34 C.F.R. § 104.44(c) (2004).

[xix] 34 C.F.R. § 104.44(d)(2) (2004).

[xx] 28 C.F.R. § 36.309(c)(3), (5) (2004).

[xxi] Tucker, B. (1996). Application of the Americans with Disabilities Act (ADA) and Section 504 to Colleges and Universities: An Overview and Discussion of Special Issues Relating to Students. *The Journal of College and University Law.*

Resource Guide

Liat Ben-Moshe

The following bibliography includes recent disability studies articles in selected disciplines.

For a fuller list of books, web sites, films and articles that engage with disability issues in different disciplines, access *Disability studies: Information and resources,* an online publication produced by the Center on Human Policy at Syracuse University: http://soeweb.syr.edu/thechp/Disability_Studies_2003_current.html

For more information on disability issues in postsecondary education see *Beyond compliance: An information package on the inclusion of people with disabilities in postsecondary education*, another online publication produced by the same group available at: http://soeweb.syr.edu/thechp/BCCC_PACKAGE.HTML

The print version does include reprints that cannot be re-produced on the web site. Print copies of both publications can be requested by writing to:

Center on Human Policy
Syracuse University
805 S. Crouse Ave.
Syracuse, NY 13244-2280 or by calling the center at
(315) 443-3851 or (800) 894-0826.

Disability Studies Articles

Anthropology

Colligan, S. (2001). The ethnographers body as text and context: Revisiting and revisioning the body through anthropology and disability studies. *Disability Studies Quarterly 21(3)*.

Kasnitz, D. & Shuttleworth, R. (2001). Anthropology anddisability studies. In L. Rogers & B. Swadener (Eds.), *Semiotics and dis/ability: Interrogating categories of difference* (pp. 1941). Albany, NY: SUNY Press.

Kasnitz, D. & Shuttleworth, R. (Eds.) (2001, Summer). Theme: Engaging Anthropology in Disability Studies [Special issue]. *Disability Studies Quarterly, 21(3)*, 217.

Shuttleworth, R. and Kasnitz, D. (2003). Special topics in social/cultural anthropology: Anthropology & disability. In L. Schlesinger & D. Taub (Eds.), *Instructional materials for sociology and disability studies*. Albany, N.Y.: SUNY Press.

Willett, J. & Deegan, M.J. (2001). Liminality and disability: Rites of passage and community in hypermodern society. *Disability Studies Quarterly, 21(3)*, 137-152.

Bioethics

Amundson, R. (2000). Against Normal Function. *Studies in History and Philosophy of Biological and Biomedical Sciences*, 31(1): 33-53.

Andrews, L., & Hibbert, M. (2000). Courts and wrongful birth: Can disability itself be viewed as a legal wrong? In L. Francis & A. Silvers (Eds.), *Americans with disabilities: Exploring implications of the law for individuals and institutions* (pp. 318-330). New York: Routledge.

Asch, A. (2000). Why I haven't changed my mind about prenatal diagnosis: Reflections and refinements. In E. Parens & A. Asch (Eds.), *Parental testing and disability rights* (pp. 234-258). Washington, D.C.: Georgetown University Press.

Bickenbach, J. (1998). Disability and life-ending decisions. In M. Battin, R. Rhodes & A. Silvers (Eds.), *Physician-assisted suicide: Expanding the debate* (pp. 123-132). New York: Routledge.

Brock, D. (2000). Health care resource prioritization and discrimination against persons with disabilities. In L. Francis & A. Silvers (Eds.), *Americans with disabilities: Exploring implications of the law for individuals and institutions* (pp. 223-235). New York: Routledge.

Buchanan, A. (1996). Choosing who will be disabled: Genetic intervention and the morality of inclusion. *Social Philosophy and Policy, 13(2)*, 18-46.

Green, R. (1997). Prenatal autonomy and the obligation not to harm one's child genetically. *Journal of law, medicine and ethics*, 25, 5-15.

Groce, N. E., Chamie, M. & Me, A. (1999). Measuring the quality of life: Rethinking the World Banks's disability adjusted life years. *International Rehabilitation Review*, 49(1 & 2): 12-15.

Jennings, B. (2000). Technology and the genetic imaginary: Prenatal testing and the construction of disability. In E. Parens & A. Asch (Eds.), *Parental testing and disability rights* (pp. 124-144). Washington, D.C.: Georgetown University Press.

Pfeiffer, D. (1994). Eugenics and Disability Discrimination. *Disability & Society*, 9(4): 481-99.

Rock, P. J. (1996). Eugenics and Euthanasia: A cause for concern for disabled people, Particularly disabled women. *Disability & Society*, 11(1, March): 121-127.

Silvers, A. (1998). Protecting the innocents from physician-assisted suicide. In M. Battin, R. Rhodes, & A. Silvers (Eds.), *Physician-assisted suicide: Expanding the debate* (pp. 133-148). New York: Routledge.

Silvers, Anita. (1995). Reconciling Equality to Difference: Caring (f)or Justice for People with Disabilities. *Hypatia*, 10(1): 30-55.

Composition and Rhetoric

Brueggemann, B., Cheu, J., Dunn, P. A., Feldmeier-White, L. & Heifferon, B. A. (2001). Becoming visible: Lessons in disability. *College Composition and Communication,* 52(3), 368-98.

Barber-Fendley, K. & Hamel, C. (2004). A new visibility: An argument for alternative assistance writing programs for students with learning disabilities. *College Composition and Communication,* 55(3).

Brueggemann, B. (2001). An enabling pedagogy: Meditations on writing and disability. *JAC: Journal of Advanced Composition,* 21(4), 791-820.

Lewiecki-Wilson, C., (2001). Doing the right thing vs. disability rights: A response to Ellen Barton. *JAC: Journal of Advanced Composition,* 21(4).

McRuer, R. (2004). Composing bodies; or, de-composition: Queer theory, disability studies, and alternative corporealities" *JAC: Journal of Advanced Composition,* 24(1).

Morse, T. A., Lewiecki-Wilson, C., Lindblom, K., Dunn, P. A., Brueggemann, B., Kleege, G., Stremlau, T. M., Erin, J., & Wilson, J. C. (2003). Symposium: Representing disability rhetorically [Special issue]. *Rhetoric Review*, 22(2), 154-202.

Drama

Disability and Performance [Special issue]. (2001, summer) *Contemporary Theatre Review*, 11.

Garland-Thomson, R. (2000). Staring Back: Self-representations of disabled performance artists. *American Quarterly*, 52(2): 334-38.

Education

Gabel S. & Danforth S. (Eds.) (2004, Spring). Theme: Education and Disability Studies [Special issue]. *Disability Studies Quarterly*. 24(2)

Baker, B. (2002). The hunt for disability: The new eugenics and the normalization of school children. *Teachers College Record*, 104(4), 663-703.

Davis, L., & Linton, S. (1995, Fall). Disability Studies [Special issue]. *Radical Teacher*, No. 47.

Erickson, K. A. (2000). All children are ready to learn: An emergent versus readiness perspective in early literacy assessment. *Seminars in Speech and Language*, 21(3), 193-203.

Gabel, S. (Ed.). (2001). "I wash my face with dirty water": Narratives of disability and pedagogy. *Journal of Teacher Education*, 52(1), 31-47.

Giangreco, M. F., Luiselli, T. E, & MacFarland, S. Z. C. (1997). Helping or hovering? Effects of instructional assistant proximity on students with disabilities. *Exceptional Children,* 64:1, 7-18.

Hehir, T. (2002, Spring). Eliminating ableism in education. *Harvard Education Review, 72(1).*

Kliewer, C. & Biklen, D. (2001). "School's not really a place for reading": A research synthesis of the literate lives of students with severe disabilities. *JASH,* 26(1), 1-12.

Ware, L.P. (2001). Writing, identity, and the other: Dare we do disability studies? *Journal of Teacher Education,* 52(2), 107-123.

Watts, I.E. & Erevelles, N. (2004). These deadly times: Reconceptualizing school violence by using critical race theory and disability studies. *American Educational Research Journal,* 41(2), 271-299.

Engineering and students with disabilities

The higher education academy engineering subject centre. Loughborough University. Available on the World Wide Web: http://www.ltsneng.ac.uk/er/dis/index.asp

Hopkins, C, Jackson, D., Tennant, J. & Wilson, A. (2002). *LTSN engineering guide: Working with disabilities.* Loughborough University. Available on the World Wide Web: http://www.ltsneng.ac.uk/downloads/disability_Guide_web.pdf

Exact sciences

Amundson, R. (2000). Against normal function. *Studies in History and Philosophy of Biological and Biomedical Sciences,* 31(C), 33-53.

Amundson, R. (2000). Biological normality and the ADA. In L. Pickering Francis & A. Silvers (Eds.), *Americans with disabilities: Exploring implications of the law for individuals and institutions* (pp. 102-110). New York: Routledge.

Hopkins, C. (1999). *Disabled person: Able scientist, technologist.* England: Nottingham Trent University.

Rousso, H. (1997). Seeing the world anew: Science and disability. In N. Kreinberg & E. Wahl (Eds.), *Thoughts and needs: Equity in mathematics and science education.* American Association for the Advancement of Science.

Geography

Butler, R. & Bowlby, S. (1997). Bodies and spaces: an exploration of disabled people's experiences of public space. *Environment and Planning D: Society and Space,* 15, 411-433.

Butler, R. (1999). Double the trouble or twice the fun? Disabled bodies in the gay community. In R. Butler & H. Parr (Eds.), *Mind and body spaces: Geographies of illness, impairment and disability* (pp. 203-220). London and New York: Routledge.

Chouinard, V. (1997). Making space for disabling differences: Challenging ableist geographies. *Environment and Planning D: Society and Space,* 15(4), 379-386.

Chouinard, V. (1999). Being out of place: Disabled women's explorations of ableist spaces. In E. Teather (Ed.), *Embodied geographies: spaces, bodies and rites of passage.* London and New York: Routledge.

Chouinard, V. (1999). Life at the margins: disabled women's explorations of ableist spaces. In E. K. Teather (Ed.), *Embodied geographies: Spaces, bodies and rites of passage* (pp. 142-156). London & New York: Routledge.

Chouinard, V. (2002). What's My Life Got to Do with Yours?: Why Disability is Every Woman's Issue. In P. Downe & L. Biggs (Eds.), *Reader in women's studies.* Nova Scotia: Fernwood Press.

Chouinard, V. & Crooks, V. (2003). Disability in Society and Space. *Canadian Geographer,* 47(4).

Dorn, M., & Metzel, D. (Eds.) (2001, Fall). Theme: Disability geography: Commonalities in a world of differences [Special issue]. *Disability Studies Quarterly,* 21(4).

Gleeson, B. (2000). Disability and the Open City. *Urban Studies,* 38(2): 251-65.

Imrie, R. (2000). Disabling Environments and the Geography of Access Policies and Practices. *Disability & Society,* 15(1): 5- 24.

Imrie, R. (2001). Barriered and bounded places and the spatialities of disability. *Urban Studies,* 38(2), 231-237.

Kitchin, R. (1998). "Out of place," "knowing one's place": Towards a spatialised theory of disability and social exclusion. *Disability and Society,* 13(3): 343-356.

Kitchin, R. (1999). Creating an awareness of Others: Highlighting the role of space and place. *Geography,* 84(1), 45-54.

Kitchin, R. (1999). Ethics and morals in geographical studies of disability. In J. Proctor & D. Smith (Eds.), *Geography and ethics: Journeys through a moral terrain* (pp. 223-236). London & New York: Routledge.

Kitchin, R. & Wilton, R. (Eds.). (2000). Disability, Geography and Ethics [Special issue]. *Ethics, Place and Environment,* 3(1): 61- 102.

Kitchin, R. (2001). Disability and inclusive landscapes. *Teaching Geography,* 26(2), 81-85.

Kitchin, R. & Law, R. (2001). The socio-spatial construction of disabled-access toilets. *Urban Studies,* 32, 287-298.

Metzel, D. & Dorn, M., (2004, Summer). Theme: Disability & Geography II [Special issue]. *Disability Studies Quarterly,* 24(3).

Park, D. C., Radford, J. P., & Vickers, M. H. (1998). Disability studies in human geography. *Progress in Human Geography,* 22(2), 208-233.

Stienstra, D. (2002). DisAbling globalisation: Rethinking global political economy with a disability lens. *Global Society,* 16(2), 109-121.

Wilton, R. (2000). Grounding hierarchies of acceptance: The social construction of disability in Nimby conflicts. *Urban Geography,* 21(7), 586-608.

History

Baynton, D. (2001). Disability and the justification of inequality in American history. In P. Longmore and L. Umansky, (Eds.), *The new disability history: American perspectives* (pp 33-57). New York: New York University Press.

Kudlick, C. J. (2003). Disability history: Why we need another 'Other.' *American Historical Review,* 108(3)

Longmore, P. K. & Goldberger, D. (2000). The League of the Physically Handicapped and the Great Depression: A Case Study in the New Disability History. *Journal of American History,* 87(3), 888-922.

Instructional design

Burgstahler, S. (2001). Universal design of instruction. *DO-IT Web site*. University of Washington. Available on The World Wide Web: http://www.washington.edu/doit

Meyer, A. & Rose, D. H. (2000). Universal design for individual differences. *Educational Leadership, 58*(3), 39-43.

Orkwis, R. (2003). Universally designed instruction. *ERIC Clearinghouse on Disabilities and Gifted Education.* Available on the World Wide Web: http://ericed.org

Pisha, B. & Coyne, P. (2001). Smart from the start: The promise of universal design for learning. *Remedial and Special Education, 22*(4), 197-203.

Law and policy

Bagenstos, S. R. (2000) Subordination, Stigma, and "Disability." *Virginia Law Review*, 86(3): 397-534.

Batavia, A. I. & Schriner, K. (2001). The Americans with Disabilities Act as engine of social change: Models of disability and the potential of a Civil Rights approach. *Policy Studies Journal,* 29(4), 690-702.

Blanck, P. D., Millender, M. (2000). Before disability civil rights: Civil War pensions and the politics of Disability in America. *Alabama Law Review*, 52(1).

Blanck P. & Schartz, H. (Eds.) (2005). Corporate Culture and Disability [Special issue]. *Behavioral Sciences and the Law,* 23(1).

Burkhauser, R. V. & Daly, M. C. (1996). The potential impact on the employment of people with disabilities. In J. West (Ed.), *Implementing the Americans with Disabilities Act* (pp. 153-191). Cambridge, MA: Milbank Memorial Fund, Blackwell.

Burkhauser, R. V. (1997). Post-ADA: Are people with disabilities expected to work? *The Annals of the American Academy of Political and Social Science*, 549 (January), 71-83.

Finkelstein, V. (1993). Disability: A social challenge or an administrative responsibility. In Swain, J., Finkelstein V., French S. and Oliver, M. (Eds) *Disabling Barriers- Enabling Environments.* London: Sage and Open University Press

Mayerson, A. B. & Mayer, K. S. (2000). Defining disability in the aftermath of Sutton. Where do we go from here? *Human Rights*, Vol. 27, No 1: A publication of the American Bar Association.

O'Day, B., Schartz H. and Blanck P. (Eds.) (2002). Disability, public policy and employment [Special issue]. *Behavioral Sciences and the Law*, 20(6)

O'Day, B., Schartz H. and Blanck P. (Eds.) (2003). Disability, Public Policy and Employment [Special issue]. *Behavioral Sciences and the Law*, 21(1)

Russell, M. (2000). Backlash, the Political Economy, and Structural Exclusion. *Berkeley Journal of Employment and Labor Law*, 21(1): 335-66.

Scotch, R. (2000). Models of Disability and the Americans with Disabilities Act. *Berkeley Journal of Employment and Labor Law*, 21(1): 213-22.

Scotch, R. (2001). American disability policy in the twentieth century. In Longmore, P. and Umansky, L. (Eds) *The New Disability History: American Perspectives*. New York: NYU Press

Scotch, R. & Schriner, K. (1997). Disability as human variation: Implications for policy. *Annals of the American Academy of Political and Social Science*; Thousand Oaks

Silverstein, R. (2000). Emerging Disability policy framework: A guidepost for analyzing public policy. *Iowa Law Review*, 85(5): 1691-1806.

Philosophy

Kittay, E. F. & Gottlieb, R. (Eds.) (2001, October). Embodied values: Philosophy and disabilities [Special issue]. *Social Theory and Practice: An International Journal of Social Philosophy*, 27 (4)

Psychology

Beresford, P. (2000). What have madness and psychiatric system survivors got to do with disability and disability studies? *Disability & Society*, 15(1): 167-72.

Olkin, R. & Pledger, C. (2003, April). Can Disability Studies and Psychology Join Hands? *American Psychologist*.

Marks, D (ed.) (2002, Summer). Theme: Counseling, Therapy, and Emancipatory Praxis [Special issue]. *Disability Studies Quarterly*, 22(3)

Roach, A. T. (2003). In search of a paradigm shift: What disability studies can contribute to school psychology. *Disability Studies Quarterly*, 23 (3/4)

Queer studies

Atkins, D. & Marston, C. (1999). Creating accessible queer community: Intersections and fractures with dis/ability praxis. *Journal of Gay, Lesbian, and Bisexual Identity*, 4(1), 3-21.

Butler, R. (1999). Double the trouble or twice the fun? Disabled bodies in the gay community. In R. Butler & H. Parr (Eds.), *Mind and body spaces: Geographies of illness, impairment and disability* (pp. 203-220). London and New York: Routledge.

Samuels, E. (2003). My body, my closet: Invisible disability and the limits of coming-out discourse. *GLQ: A Journal of Lesbian and Gay Studies*, 9(1-2), 233-255.

Tremain, S. (Ed.). (1998, Summer). Theme, Disability studies queered [Special issue]. *Disability Studies Quarterly,* 18(3).

McRuer, R. & Wilkerson, A. (Eds.). (2003). Desiring disability: Queer theory meets disability studies [Special issue]. *GLQ: A Journal of Lesbian and Gay Studies,* 9(1-2), 233-255.

Sociology

Barnes, C. (1998). The social model of disability: A sociological phenomenon ignored by sociologists? In T. Shakespeare (Ed.), *The disability reader*. London: Continuum.

Gordon, B. & Rosenblum, K. (2001). Bringing disability into the sociological frame: A comparison of disability with race, sex and sexual orientation statuses. *Disability & Society*, 16(1), 5-19.

Oliver, M. (1995). The sociology of liberation. Available on the World Wide Web: http://www.leeds.ac.uk/disability-studies/archiveuk/Oliver/hull%20seminar.pdf

Roulstone, A. (1995). Sociology as a critical and emancipatory discipline: Building a community of scholars in sociology and dis ability studies. Available on the World Wide Web: http://www.leeds.ac.uk/disability-studies/archiveuk/roulstone/ building.pdf

Scotch, R. K. (2002). Paradigms of American social research on disability: What's new? *Disability Studies Quarterly*, 22(2), 23-24.

Women's studies/ Feminist perspectives

Asch, A. & Fine, M. (1997). Nurturance, sexuality and women with disabilities: The example of women and literature. In L. J. Davis (Ed.), *The disability studies reader*. New York: Routledge.

Corker, M. (2001). Sensing disability. *Hypatia,* 16(4), 34-52.

Garland Thomson, R. (1997). Feminist theory, the body and the disabled figure. In L. J. Davis (Ed), *The disability studies reader*. New York: Routledge.

Hall, K. Q. (Ed.) (2003, Fall). Feminist Disability Studies [Special issue]. *NSWA Journal*, 14(3).

Hubbard, R. (1997). Abortion and disability: Who should and who should not inhabit the world? In L. J. Davis (Ed.), *The disability studies reader*. New York: Routledge.

Kittay, Silvers, S. & Wendell, S. (Eds.). (2001). Feminism and disability [Special issue]. *Hypatia,* 16(4).

Kittay, E., Silvers, S., & Wendell, S. (Eds.). (2002). Feminism and disability II [Special issue]. *Hypatia,* 17(3).

Schriempf, A. (2001, fall). (Re)fusing the amputated body: An interactionist bridge for feminism and disability. *Hypatia*, 16(4), 53-79.

Wendell, S. (1997). Toward a feminist theory of disability. In L. J. Davis (Ed.), *The disability studies reader*. New York: Routledge.

Contributors

Thomas Argondizza
Thomas Argondizza started working with instructional design while employed by BellSouth. He took a sabbatical leave and pursued a master's of science in instructional design, development and evaluation at Syracuse University. While at Syracuse University, he designed and developed materials for the Federal Aviation Administration, the Syracuse Information Institute and the Syracuse City School District. He is currently employed as an instructional designer in Maryland.

Katrina Arndt
Katrina Arndt is a doctoral student in the special education program at Syracuse University. For the past several years, she has worked in classrooms with youth who have disabilities and has been an ally to students with disabilities. Her research interests include self-determination and self advocacy.

Christy Ashby
Christy Ashby is a graduate student at Syracuse University pursuing her doctorate in special education and in disability studies. A former inclusive special education teacher, she is interested in inclusive education at all levels with particular interest in the school experiences of students with autism and mental retardation labels. Other research interests include the social construction of disability and issues of cultural representation.

Maria Barile

Maria G. Barile received a master's degree in social work from
McGill University in 1993. She is among 17 female co-founders
of Dis-Abled Women's Network Canada and its local affiliate
Action des femmes handicapées (Montréal). As an activist, she
uses writing to promote a progressive perspective of the lives of
persons with disabilities. She works for Adaptech Research
Network ().

Liat Ben-Moshe

Liat Ben-Moshe began pursuing her doctorate in sociology,
disability studies and women's studies at Syracuse University in
2002. Her current research interests are construction of dis/Ability,
representations of disability in film and literature, discourse on
nationalism and militarization, activism and the body. She is also
an active member of Beyond Compliance (BCCC), an
organization devoted to raising awareness around disability issues
at Syracuse University.

Tammy Berberi

Tammy Berberi (doctorate, Indiana University) is an assistant
professor of French at the University of Minnesota in Morris,
where she also directs the university's Language Teaching Center.
She has advocated for students and educators with disabilities for
more than a decade and currently serves as the moderator of
DS-HUM, a listserv devoted to disability in the humanities.

Jeremy L. Brunson

Jeremy has been a sign language interpreter for 10 years and has
taught interpreters for 5 years. He holds a certification of
interpretation and a certification of transliteration from the
Registry of Interpreters for the Deaf. A native of Arizona, he is
currently pursuing sociology and disability studies in the graduate
school of Syracuse University. His current research focus is the
transformation process of sign language interpreting as it moves
from something people "do" (an occupation) to something people
"are" (a profession).

Rebecca C. Cory

Rebecca Cory is a doctoral candidate in cultural foundations of education and disability studies at Syracuse University. She works as the disability specialist at Wells College and is a founding member of Beyond Compliance (BCCC).

Crystal Doody

Crystal Doody is a third-year, joint-degree student in law and disability studies. She is a founding member of the disAbility Law Society. In May of 2005, she will be among the first graduates of the combined juris doctorate/ master's of science in education program at Syracuse University. Crystal hopes to work as a disability rights attorney while also using her degree to educate attorneys about people with disabilities and to educate people with disabilities about legal advocacy.

Pat English-Sand

Pat English-Sand is a teacher of students with special needs, an inclusion facilitator and an ally to students and colleagues with disabilities. She is also a doctoral student in special education and disability studies at Syracuse University. Her research examines the experience of students with significant disabilities in inclusive educational settings with a focus on the development of literacy skills.

Mia Feldbaum

Mia Feldbaum is a graduate student at Syracuse University pursuing her master's degree in cultural foundations of education and in disability studies. She also leads inclusive extended wilderness trips in the United States and in Canada. She is a member of Beyond Compliance (BCCC). Her research interests include the intersections of disability, race and gender; inclusive outdoor education; media representations; and international human rights.

Elizabeth Hamilton

Elizabeth Hamilton is an assistant professor of German at Oberlin College. Her research explores discourses of disability in German literature, film and foreign language pedagogy. She has also served on the executive committee of the Disability Studies Discussion Group within the Modern Language Association.

Anita Ho

Anita Ho is an assistant professor of philosophy and a co-coordinator of the Center for Women, Economic Justice and Public Policy at The College of St. Catherine in St. Paul, Minnesota. Her teaching and research interests include disability issues, ethics, bioethics and business ethics as well as social and political philosophy.

Kathy Kniepmann

Kathy Kniepmann is on the faculty of the Washington University School of Medicine in St. Louis. She teaches disability courses for undergraduates and teaches health promotion, culture and community education for graduate students. She is an occupational therapist and health educator. Her master's degrees in education and public health are from Harvard University where she developed an office of health education for students, faculty and staff. Her interests include disability studies, media effects, social change and cross-cultural issues in health.

Ann Millett

Ann Millett is a doctoral candidate at the University of North Carolina at Chapel Hill. She is currently working on a dissertation that combines the disciplines of art history and disability studies, focusing on examples of contemporary art that relate to historical venues that place the disabled body on display.

Julie Morse

Julie Morse is a third-year, joint-degree student in law and disability studies. She is a founding member of the disAbility Law Society. In May of 2005, she will be among the first graduates of the combined juris doctorate/ master's of science in education program at Syracuse University. Julie hopes to work as a disability rights attorney while also using her degree to educate attorneys about people with disabilities and to educate people with disabilities about legal advocacy.

Cheryl G. Najarian

Cheryl G. Najarian is an assistant professor of sociology and a faculty associate in the Center for Women and Work at the University of Massachusetts, Lowell. She received her bachelor's in English from Boston College, her master's in higher education administration from the University of Arizona and her doctorate in sociology from Syracuse University. Her current research investigates the mothering and paid-work experiences of college-educated deaf women in two different geographical locations. She teaches introductory courses in sociology and gender studies.

Anthony J. Nocella, II

Anthony J. Nocella, II is a social science doctoral student at the Maxwell School of Syracuse University. He holds a M.A. in Peacemaking and Conflict Studies from Fresno Pacific University. Nocella a long-time peace, animal rights, mentally challenged, and environmental activist, first became involved in political activism while attending the Delaware Valley Friends School in Philadelphia, PA, a private Quaker school for students with learning differences. He later moved with his family to Houston, Texas and graduated from Briarwood High School (a private school for mentally and learning challenged students), as the Student of the Year and was awarded the Presidential Award from President Clinton.

Sara Pace

Sara Pace is working on her doctorate in rhetoric at Texas Woman's University, where she also teaches composition and literature courses. Her dissertation focuses on the use of voice recognition software as a writing tool for writers at the college level.

Michele Paetow

Michele Paetow has a master's degree in special education from Syracuse University and has taught at every grade level in her 30-year career in the Syracuse and Oswego schools. Her interests include expanding the ways schools, including colleges, provide instruction and develop an accepting and respectful community for diverse learners, including those with autism and severe disabilities.

Zach Rosetti

Zach Rossetti is currently pursuing a doctorate in special education and in disability studies at Syracuse University. He is a former teacher and inclusion facilitator from New Hampshire. His research interests include inclusive education, autism, friendship formation and media representations of disability. He is a huge Boston Red Sox fan.

Ken Sagendorf

Ken Sagendorf is an associate director for Professional Development Programs of the Graduate School at Syracuse University. He is an adjunct instructor in exercise science as well as a doctoral candidate in science teaching. His research involves studying faculty members in their first year on the job.

Elizabeth Sierra-Zarella

Elizabeth Sierra-Zarella, a third-year doctoral student in child and family studies, was born and raised in Wichita Falls, Texas. As a first-generation college student from an impoverished family, a Hispanic woman with multiple disabilities, and a former teen mother on welfare, she has faced oppression on many levels and is committed to identifying and removing the societal barriers preventing people from reaching their highest potential. She currently resides in Camillus, New York, with her husband, Mark, and her daughter, Tabitha.

Julia White

Julia White is a doctoral candidate in the special education and disability studies programs at Syracuse University. Her research interests include inclusive education for social justice, especially for students of ethnic minorities; comparative analyses of special education law; and disability studies, especially as it pertains to popular culture.